MW01031900

A POCKET HISTORY OF THE

IRISH
FAMINE

Gill Books
Hume Avenue, Park West, Dublin 12

www.gillbooks.ie

Gill Books is an imprint of M.H. Gill & Co.

Copyright © Teapot Press Ltd 2018

ISBN: 978-0-7171-7944-2

This book was created and produced by Teapot Press Ltd

Text by Fiona Biggs
Designed by Tony Potter

Printed in the EU

This book is typeset in Dax, Minion and Albertus

A CIP catalogue record for this book is available
from the British Library.

5 4 3 2 1

A POCKET HISTORY OF THE
IRISH
FAMINE

FIONA BIGGS

Gill Books

Contents

Introduction

Throughout her history, Ireland, like much of Europe and other parts of the world, was plagued by periodic outbreaks of famine caused by crop failure. These famines were frequently localised and of a relatively short duration. The Great Irish Famine, *an Gorta Mór,* was something very different. When the potato blight struck in 1845, the poor rural population of Ireland was almost completely dependent on the potato – when the potato crop was blighted in successive years, starvation on an enormous scale was the inevitable outcome. One million people died of hunger and the diseases associated with starvation, while a further million emigrated to England and the territories of the New World. Although there were further crop failures in Ireland in the years that followed the Great Famine, the power of the word 'famine' was such that it was never again used by the authorities to describe situations of food shortage or crop failure.

The Great Famine was shocking not simply because of the cause (it is difficult to conceive of the entire poor population of a nation subsisting on a single food crop), but because of the callousness of the administration's paltry response to it. The famine was not in some far-flung outpost of the British Empire, but in England's neighbouring island, Britain's oldest colony. For most of the Irish gentry and landed nobility life went on as normal while people died by the roadsides in their thousands. Irish politicians had other fish to fry and largely ignored the tragedy that was unfolding on their doorsteps. This failure to act is incomprehensible from a 21st-century perspective, when governments are expected to provide financial and practical aid to their citizens in times of difficulty.

However, in Victorian Britain, things were very different. The doctrine of laissez-faire was the guiding principle of social administration and encouraged a position that was the polar opposite of today's so-called 'nanny state'. The Poor Law, first instituted in 1601 in the reign of Queen Elizabeth I, was the only system of relief available to the poor. It had been established to provide assistance to the agricultural poor and, even with later refinements, was ill-suited to the industrial landscape of Victorian Britain, where people lived in abject poverty in appalling living conditions. The idea that the poor were poor because of their own moral failings took hold in the popular

THE POTATO EATERS
Vincent Van Gogh
Van Gogh
Museum,
Amsterdam

imagination – there was therefore no moral requirement to help them. Charity was almost the only recourse of the poor and was generally provided by those of less rigid beliefs.

Far from being a form of government assistance, the Poor Law was paid for by a rate levied on landowners – tenant poverty led to dwindling rents during the Famine and meant that many Irish landowners were not in a position to pay the rate. Some of the assistance provided under the Poor Law was 'indoor relief', that is in a workhouse or poorhouse, an institution deliberately designed to be the worst option available to people, no matter how abject their circumstances. The situation in Ireland was compounded by the harsh portrayal of the Irish poor in the British press – articles and cartoons lampooned them as dirty, improvident and indolent, and therefore unworthy of rescue in their hour of great need.

The Great Famine coincided with a policy of land reform that required arable land to be cleared in favour of pasture. Inability to pay the rent frequently led to eviction, and a callous amendment to the Irish Poor Law legislation required people with smallholdings of more than a quarter of an acre to give them up in order to qualify for Poor Law assistance. Consequently, the desired land reform was achievable with a minimum of investment. Charles Trevelyan, the civil servant charged with administering famine relief in Ireland, believed that God had sent the famine to punish the feckless Irish and was convinced that posterity would acknowledge that 'supreme Wisdom has educed permanent good out of transient evil'.

The Great Famine has had a lasting effect on the nation. Emigration continued year on year, finally tailing off in the 1990s, producing a worldwide diaspora of some 70 million people, recognised in Article 2 of the Irish Constitution as those 'people of Irish ancestry living abroad who share its cultural identity and heritage', many of whom have a visceral connection with Ireland and its history. The Great Famine seems destined to be forever etched on the psyche of Irish people everywhere – the collective 'folk memory' of the dreadful years of devastation will not allow it to be forgotten.

A Remarkably Nutritious Food

These roots are round, some as large as a walnut, others much larger; they grow in damp soil, many hanging together as if fixed with ropes. They are good food, whether boiled or roasted.

Thomas Heriot, 1578

The potato was first brought to Europe by the Spanish in 1537 – when they encountered the unremarkable tuber during their conquest of the Incan Empire in South America they were initially unimpressed. They confused it with the sweet potato, *batata*, and this initial confusion led to the potato retaining a vestige of the name of the other root. However, despite the early scepticism of the conquistadors, they had soon realised the potato's potential as a highly nutritious foodstuff that would keep well during long voyages. It also seemed to have properties that aided in the prevention of scurvy, the scourge of sailors.

Having sustained themselves on the potato during the voyage back to Europe, the returning conquistadors introduced it to Spain. People weren't sure how to eat it – cooking didn't seem to have occurred to them – and disliked the bitter taste of the raw tuber. The potato didn't gain widespread acceptance until it had been experimented with and cooked in a variety of ways. By the early 1600s, it had travelled to Italy, Portugal, Austria, Holland, Belgium, France, Switzerland, Germany and England. Those who cultivated it in Spain found that it grew particularly well in the harsh conditions of the Atlantic seaboard; its chief appeal has always been its adaptability to poor soil and difficult terrain so it was ideally suited to the west of Ireland.

However, despite its usefulness as a cheap, easy-to-grow food source, a good deal of superstition surrounded the potato and its cultivation. Because it isn't mentioned in the Bible and is grown in what was acknowledged to be Satan's realm under the ground, it was often associated with witchcraft and

FLOWERS
of the potato plant

THE POTATO HARVEST

Jean-François Millet, 1855 (Walters Art Museum)

the devil. Owing to the fact that it was discovered to belong to the same family as deadly nightshade it was believed to be poisonous. In fact, potatoes at the time did contain significantly larger amounts of the poisonous chemical solanum than they do today, and ingestion of a significant quantity could produce a nasty, albeit temporary, rash. Even in Ireland, where they became so important, potatoes are still traditionally planted on Good Friday and sprinkled with holy water to avert evil.

According to tradition, the potato was first introduced to Ireland by the great English adventurer Sir Walter Raleigh after his third expedition to the Americas in 1584. Legend has it that he stopped off in Ireland on his return journey from Virginia (named after Queen Elizabeth I, referred to as the Virgin Queen by the poet Edmund Spenser) and distributed the remains of his potato cargo to the native population there, but this story has no foundation in fact. Although Raleigh organised and received sponsorship for no fewer

SIR WALTER RALEIGH
attributed to William Segar (1564-1633) 1598

than nine expeditions to the New World, he himself accompanied only the first of these, and that had to turn back before it reached the shores of Virginia. When Raleigh brought the potato to Ireland, probably in 1586, it is unlikely that he introduced it as a completely new species. The potato had been introduced to continental Europe by Spain, but in England and Ireland, because of the Raleigh connection, it was referred to as 'the Virginia potato'. Raleigh is known to have grown it on his estate at Myrtle Grove, Youghal, County Cork, a gift from the queen for his role in the brutal suppression of the Desmond rebellions.

In the second half of the 16th century Queen Elizabeth had tried to increase her power and influence in the south of Ireland, where the population had so far resisted all efforts to subdue it. Her armies were met with fierce resistance from the Earl of Desmond, whose family had ruled much of Munster for more than three centuries. There were two Desmond rebellions against the English power

GERALD FITZGERALD, 15th Earl of Desmond

MAP OF IRELAND
c.1570. The Desmonds ruled the southwest corner of the island.

grab, the first lasting from 1569 to 1573. England took a conciliatory approach in its wake. However, soon afterwards the rebels looked for Catholic help from the Continent and a second rebellion, backed by a papal contingent, was launched in 1579. It was brutally quashed by the English forces – by 1583 the province was devastated, with tens of thousands of people, including civilians, dead, and thousands more displaced. The Annals of the Four Masters reported that in the aftermath of the fighting, 'the lowing of a cow, or the whistle of the ploughboy, could scarcely be heard from Dunquinn [sic] to Cashel in Munster'.

After the failure of the rebellions, the Crown claimed 600,000 acres of Desmond land in Munster as forfeit, and parcelled it out to so-called 'gentlemen undertakers' who were required to populate their estates with Englishmen within a set time period. It was hoped that a large English population would have the effect of subduing the native people, thus preventing any further insurrection. Raleigh was one

DESMOND CASTLE
in Kinsale, County Cork

of the gentleman undertakers, being gifted 42,000 acres of the forfeited land in Cork and Waterford. His success in attracting Englishmen to settle his land was qualified, but he is known to have planted potatoes as a garden crop on his land, following the fashion of the times for planting crops as botanical specimens.

If the potato had become prolific immediately after its introduction to Ireland, it might have helped to mitigate the effects of the post-rebellion food shortages that resulted from the damage to the land during the fighting. However, even 140 years later the potato was still not an important food crop. Contemporary reports of food shortages in the first quarter of the 18th century make it clear that bread, usually made from corn, was still the staple of the poor in Ireland.

By that time a tax, or tithe, had been introduced on the production of most crops, including hops, flax, hemp and turnips. The potato does not appear on the list and it may have been this tithe-free status that led to its increased cultivation. A separate agricultural development may also have contributed to the popularity of the potato among the poorest. Landowners had begun to move from tillage to livestock, a far more prosperous endeavour that required large tracts of pasture. The care of cattle and sheep required few people and large numbers of farm workers were driven away from the fertile lowlands to the mountainous areas and bogs. Very little would grow in these areas except the potato,

LAZY BEDS on Inishglora island off the Mullet Peninsula, Erris, County Mayo

which was actually very well adapted to the poor growing conditions. With the new emphasis on grazing there was no longer enough land under tillage to grow the corn that fed the nation, so reliance on the potato began to increase. It was discovered that the yield per acre of potatoes was around four times that of oats and other grain crops, with the inevitable result that many people stopped growing oats altogether, or grew just a small quantity as a cash crop with which to pay the rent.

Potatoes lent themselves to being grown in the 'lazy beds' that had been used for the cultivation of oats. It was a potato-growing method that had also been used by the Incas in Peru. The seed potatoes were laid in a row on top of the earth and were then covered with earth dug from either side of the row, creating deep channels. The covering earth was mixed with seaweed, manure, or whatever form of fertiliser was available locally. The channels that were created during the construction of the rows provided essential drainage. As the potato increased in popularity, lazy beds were increasingly utilised, and by 1740 it had become the practice to leave the tubers in the ground, covered with a fresh layer of earth, until late December each year, at which time they were dug up and stored overground until they had all been eaten.

THE POTATO DIGGERS
Paul Henry,
1876–1958

The poorest of the poor lived on potatoes and buttermilk, with coastal dwellers enjoying an occasional herring. While it lacked variety, this diet had a high nutritional content, and those depending on it had a greatly reduced risk of scurvy, rickets or the other prevalent ailments caused by low vitamin and mineral intake. The potato supplies complex carbohydrates and a small amount of protein. If the skins are eaten it is high in vitamin C, potassium, iron, magnesium and fibre. The buttermilk that usually accompanied a meal of potatoes provided calcium, together with vitamins A and D.

Meanwhile, the introduction of navigation laws that required all shipments from the English colonies to be received and taxed in England before being transported to Ireland reduced the national income, as did a prohibition on the manufacture of wool. The landowners were getting richer, while the general population was sinking into poverty and destitution. Because pasture had supplanted tillage hardly any of the food needed by the nation could be grown

in Ireland. To import food was expensive and was largely precluded by the reduced circumstances of the population. Many commentators condemned the practice of grazing at the expense of tillage, although any publicly voiced disquiet about the difficulties being experienced by the people related exclusively to those Protestant English who had settled in Ireland. There was widespread concern that that sector of the Irish population was solving the problem with emigration. The limited diet of potatoes was not acceptable to the English settlers, no matter how reduced their circumstances. A famine in 1728, which was the unavoidable result of three bad harvests in a row, provoked food riots in Munster when the available corn in the area was bought up to feed Northern Protestants. The Anglican primate of Ireland expressed his disquiet that the emigration consequent upon the famine 'affects only the Protestants'. This would have been a concern to the administration, as the very people who had been sent to keep order and pre-empt rebellion were leaving the country in droves.

The native Catholic population, many of whom had been exiled to the barren uplands to accommodate the grazing practices of their landlords, was not worthy of mention, except as an existential threat. It was not the last time their well-being would be ignored.

COUNTY DONEGAL
An Port, a deserted village

The Famine of 1740–41

The most miserable scene of universal distress – scarcely a house in the whole island escaped from tears and mourning.

Contemporary eyewitness report

Between 1720 and 1740 the country experienced 12 poor harvests and, as far as the authorities were concerned, emigration of English Protestants was becoming problematic. Then, in the winter of 1739–40, disaster struck. In the middle of December 1739, after weeks of cold, wet and windy weather, there was a hard frost throughout Europe, which set in before the potatoes had been harvested. Following tried and tested practice, the potatoes had been stored in the ground with a protective layer of earth and straw to protect them from normal weather conditions. The frost was the most severe in living memory and the protective layer of straw was unequal to its rigours. Known variously as the 'great frost', 'black frost' or 'hard frost', it destroyed the entire potato crop, including the seed potatoes for future planting, leaving the poor with no means of feeding themselves. Almost the only food crop that survived the extreme cold was the parsnip. Ironically, the 1739 potato crop had been more than usually abundant and, if harvested in time, would have provided plenty of food until the following summer.

That winter is still the coldest winter on record. The frost continued for more than two months. It was so cold that birds fell dead from the trees and the rivers froze over. They were turned into temporary highways and fairs and other gatherings were set up on the ice. Even the prawns in Dublin Bay froze to death, destroying the market for them for years to come. Incoming ships could not approach

WINTER LANDSCAPE WITH SKATERS AND A BIRD TRAP
Pieter Bruegel the Elder

the harbours with their cargoes, and vessels containing goods for export were unable to leave the quays where they were moored. The all-important coal deliveries could not be landed and the freezing poor stripped the countryside of any vegetation that could be burned for warmth.

Trees and other vegetation were destroyed by the extreme conditions. There were reports that the wool fell off the sheep and the creatures froze to death as a result. The moving parts in the flour mills seized up so no grain could be ground, depriving the people of one of their most important food sources. By the middle of January 1740 starvation was rife and subscriptions were set up so that charitable donations could be made to alleviate the suffering. Some landlords gave money and food to their tenants, but such acts of generosity and humanity were few and far between. Despite the extreme hardship experienced by the population the government took no action to

POVERTY-STRICKEN
workers

provide relief, although the Lord Lieutenant of Ireland, the Duke of Devonshire, having unsuccessfully prevailed upon the government to provide assistance, donated some of his own money to the starving and banned the export of corn for the duration of the emergency.

With most pre-industrial manufacturing machinery disabled by the extreme cold, much of the employment that was usually available to people disappeared. Providing relief work for the unemployed would have ousted other workers from their positions, so those worst affected received no assistance, apart from charity. Some benevolent landowners and other philanthropists ordered the construction of roads and canals and the cleaning of harbours in order to provide work for their tenants. While the roads, canals and harbours had some ostensible purpose, people were also put to work building 'follies'. The Killiney Obelisk, on Killiney Hill in County Dublin, was commissioned by a wealthy Catholic landowner, John Malpas. It

PORTRAIT OF WILLIAM CAVENDISH, 3rd Duke of Devonshire, K.G., by George Knapton. Three-quarter-length portrait, in a brown velvet coat with the sash and star of the Order of the Garter, seated at a table.

is the first known famine monument and can be seen from boats arriving at Dun Laoghaire harbour. The whimsical Conolly Folly in Celbridge, County Kildare, also provided work for local people. It was commissioned by Katherine Conolly, the widow of the Speaker of the House and owner of Castletown House. A couple of years later she took steps to avert hunger among her tenantry by having the Wonderful Barn built nearby to serve as a food store in the event of future famines or shortages.

CONOLLY FOLLY in Celbridge, County Kildare

As the famine worsened, some landowners helped their tenants with donations of food and money, while others held on to their grain stores, even when the Privy Council ordered the high sheriffs in each county to provide an account of all grain stocks held. Archbishop Boulter, the Irish Protestant primate, who had organised effective relief work for Northern Protestants in the famine of 1728, used his own money to provide relief, organising an emergency feeding programme for the poor of Dublin. In Drogheda, Chief Justice Henry Singleton spent much of his wealth on famine relief.

ARCHBISHOP BOULTER

At this time, the potato was still not the staple food in Ireland – it was cheap and plentiful, but grains had a more important role in the Irish diet. When the extreme cold had abated there was a two-month drought which killed many of the animals that had survived the freezing temperatures. The wheat, barley and corn crops failed and, inevitably, food prices rose – wheat trebled in price between January and August 1740. The starving people

THE RT. HON. HENRY SINGLETON
(1682–1759), Lord Chief-Justice

BARBARIC punishment was meted out to offenders.

left the land in favour of the cities, where begging was widespread. In May there was a serious bread riot in Dublin – bakers' shops were raided by large marauding bands and the bread was sold cheaply to the hungry. The rioters were rewarded with a variety of penalties, including whipping and transportation, but the Lord Mayor gave permission for foreign bakers to bake household bread, and prices came down. In other cities, including Waterford, starving people who stole food were fired on by the military. Gangs of thieves roamed the countryside – the most notorious was the Kellymount Gang, based near Kilkenny. They stole horses, sheep and money (carefully excluding 'the gentlemen of County Kilkenny' from their attentions), some of which they redistributed among the poor. A military contingent arrested many of the gang members and they were duly tried, convicted and hanged.

Although the famine continued and worsened throughout 1740 the administration's response to the suffering of the starving was inadequate, despite representations made by the Duke of Devonshire. A letter to an Irish MP presented a stark picture of the suffering of the people:

> … want and misery in every face … the roads spread with dead and dying bodies; mankind of the colour of the docks and nettles they fed on; two or three, sometimes more, going on a car to the grave for want of bearers to carry them, and many only buried in the fields and ditches where they perished.

Starvation was quickly joined by its usual companions – dysentery and fever – and the casualties soon numbered hundreds of thousands. The 'bloody flux' and 'malignant fever' were no respecters of rank, and the dead came from all echelons of society. The jails were so full that there was hardly room for the prisoners to lie down on the floor and thousands of those incarcerated in them contracted disease and died. In

DYSENTERY was rife among the starving poor.

Galway the medical professionals believed that the city had been afflicted with the plague rather than a fever and the authorities took the precaution of moving the meeting for the Galway Races further away from Galway city and closer to Terlogh Gurranes near Tuam, where the gentlefolk present were able enjoy a full programme of nightly balls and theatrical excursions.

In the autumn of 1740 there was a small grain harvest and food prices began to return to pre-famine levels. However, the extreme cold had weakened the cattle and they failed to breed in sufficient numbers to restore milk and butter production to normal levels. The faraway War of the Austrian Succession led to Spanish attacks on ships carrying grain to Ireland, and on ships from Ireland carrying the country's main exports of linen, salt beef and butter. From the end of October snow-laden blizzards devastated the east coast and they were followed by torrential rain at the beginning of December, which caused severe flooding. Small boats on the River Liffey in Dublin were wrecked by large chunks of ice tumbling through the water, while many of the larger boats that were anchored at the quays lost their moorings. The problems brought by distant war and the food shortages led to hoarding, and food prices began to increase again.

Records of mortality during the Great Frost were kept patchily, if at all. It is believed that the death rate tripled in the early months of 1740, and the burial rate increased by 50 per cent during the crisis. Conservative estimates produced a figure of 200,000 dead from famine and disease, but other reports increased that figure to almost 500,000, out of a total population of less than 2.5 million. The dead were mostly adults, which had the effect of greatly reducing the working population and creating many orphans.

When the weather finally returned to normal and the mortality rate began to reduce, the listless survivors found themselves without the strength to cultivate those small areas of land that had not been given over to pasture. Harsh penal laws were enacted against the Catholic population. The contemporary commentator Canon John O'Rourke said that the measures 'plunged the people into the deepest distress: horror and despair pervaded every mind.'

In May 1741 the Protestant Bishop of Cloyne, Dr Berkeley, wrote to a friend in Dublin:

'The distresses of the sick and poor are endless. The havoc of mankind in the counties of Cork, Limerick, and some adjacent places, hath been incredible. The nation probably will not recover this loss in a century. The other day I heard from the county of Limerick that whole villages were entirely dispeopled.'

However, in the years following the famine, growing conditions improved considerably and the national harvest had soon regained pre-famine levels. In August 1741 five shiploads of grain from America arrived in Galway, and the harvest that year, while not back to normal, was relatively good. Most importantly, with grain coming into the country, those who had been hoarding released their stocks, and food prices finally returned to normal.

After the famine, people became more dependent on the potato – it seemed less susceptible to the

PORTRAIT OF
Arthur Young
(1741–1820), British
economist and man
of letters, by
John Russell
(1745–1806)

A POTATO DINNER,
Cahirciveen, *Pictorial Times*,
28 February 1846

vagaries of the weather, guaranteeing a reliable harvest every year. With the continuing expansion of grazing, the potato was an ideal crop for growing on the small plots of poor land that were the lot of many of the native Irish. The English agricultural writer Arthur Young published his observations of the conditions he found in the Irish countryside in 1776. Despite the disastrous effects of the frost of 1739–40, people were still growing potatoes in the old way, i.e. storing them in the ground until the end of December. There were 20 times as many potatoes being cultivated as there had been in 1739. They were being fed to livestock as well as providing the main source of food for the poor, alongside milk.

Those living in coastal areas also had access to herring, and in Ulster they were able to supplement their diet with oats and a little meat. The nation was well fed on the abundant potato crop and early marriage became the norm, with the inevitable result that the population increased rapidly. Children were cheap to feed and a source of free labour for families. By 1780 the potato was the staple food of the native people of Ireland, and the type of potato cultivated was, almost exclusively, the popular 'apple' potato. The failure to diversify would have dreadful consequences.

The Famine of 1822

... better drown us than turn us off, for there is no place for us anywhere.

A plea from tenants faced with eviction from their homes in Galway, mid-1820s

By the early decades of the 19th century the potato had become more and more popular and it was increasingly relied on by the poor as a staple foodstuff. The constantly expanding population meant that growing numbers were now almost completely dependent on the simple tuber for most of their nutrition.

The spring of 1821 brought bad weather, and the heavy rain and storms delayed the potato planting that year. The inclement weather continued throughout May, and there was even frost in June, alternating with hot sunny days. The heavy rain then resumed and continued throughout the rest of the summer and the autumn of the year, causing extensive floods. Most of the crops, including potatoes, that had been sown that year were submerged under water. It was reported that 'the Shannon at Athlone looks like a boundless ocean'. The potatoes rotted in their pits. The wet weather continued through the winter and spring of 1822, and the poor harvest of the previous year meant that there were hardly any seed potatoes available for planting.

The government offered relief specific to the problems caused by the failure of the potato crop – 1,400 tons of seed potatoes were shipped to Ireland from England and Scotland to replace the stock that had been lost. Some charitable people also bought seed potatoes for distribution to those affected by the shortage – these were already chitted, or cut into 'sets', for planting in order to reduce the temptation to use them for food. Despite this precaution, many people were in such an advanced state of starvation that they dug the chitted potatoes out of the ground and ate them, which resulted in a sparse harvest.

BELL BRIDGE
(Bealaclugga Bridge) County Clare, probably built as part of famine relief work in 1822.

The counties most severely affected by the 1822 famine were Cork, Kerry, Clare, Limerick, Galway and Mayo. The price of potatoes increased by at least 400 per cent, and although grains were available for purchase, most people were too poor to buy them. Any potatoes that were available were of very inferior quality – the poor weather conditions meant that they had not ripened properly and they deteriorated further during storage. Epidemics of typhoid fever and dysentery were commonplace, and thousands of people weakened by hunger were killed by disease. A parliamentary committee set up to look into the situation reported that

FIELD ON THE WEST coast of Ireland, still showing scars of potato ridges abandoned during the famine.

> There was no want of food of another description for the support of human life; on the contrary, the crops of grain had been far from deficient, and the prices of corn and oatmeal were very moderate. The calamities of 1822 may, therefore, be said to have proceeded less from the want of food

itself, than from the want of adequate means of purchasing it; or, in other words, from the want of profitable employment.

In the west of Ireland the living were too weakened by hunger to bury the dead, and corpses piled up along the roadside. Skibbereen, in County Cork, fared worst in every famine that afflicted the Irish people – in May 1822 it was reported that the people in that locality were in a state of distress that was 'horrible beyond description'.

KILLARY, NEAR THE MOUTH OF THE BUNDORACHA RIVER,
County Galway
William Evans of Eton, 1798–1877

CHARLES STEWART PARNELL, 19th-century Irish politician, c.1874–1891. Parnell (1846–1891) was a supporter of the Irish Land League, which campaigned for land reform and against the administration of estates in Ireland by absentee landlords living in England.

The poor Catholic population was still regarded as a volatile and dangerous enemy, one that the original Protestant settlers had been sent to subdue. The huge gifts of land that had been made to these settlers meant that the local population was largely dispossessed, reduced to scraping a living from small parcels of land in the poorest and least fertile regions of the country. The owners of the large estates frequently opted for absentee status and had no concern for the welfare of their tenants, except insofar as they paid rent for their smallholdings. The agriculturalist Arthur Young observed in 1779 that

> The landlord of an Irish estate, inhabited by Roman Catholics, is a sort of despot, who yields obedience in whatever concerns the poor to no law but that of his will … A long series of oppressions, aided by very mean ill-judged laws, have brought landlords into a habit of exerting very lofty superiority, and their vassals into that of an almost

unlimited submission. Speaking a language that is despised, professing a religion that is abhorred, and being disarmed, the poor find themselves in many cases slaves even in the bosom of written liberty.

However, contrary to popular belief, it was not just the indigent Catholic Irish population that was affected by the famine. In contemporary accounts of famine in Ireland, references to the 'Irish' encompass only the Protestant colonisers, who formed about 20 per cent of the population. After the Reformation the Catholic people of Ireland were written off as 'outlaws', with no natural or civil rights. Any official expressions of outrage about the effects of famine in Ireland were usually made in respect of the English settlers only. In England, meanwhile, those same settlers, who had been given grants of land as an inducement to populate the smaller island, were viewed with suspicion and envy and many of them had been thrown into poverty by government

**PORTRAIT OF KING
WILLIAM III**
(1650–1702)
Godfrey Kneller

policies of protectionism, especially in relation to the thriving woollen industry.

By the late 1600s rural industry, particularly in the area of textile production, played an important role the Irish economy. It was also an important industry in England, which was producing a surplus of woollen goods and did not want to compete for the export market with similar goods of Irish manufacture. In 1698, at the behest of both houses of parliament, King William III promised to do all in his power to discourage Ireland's woollen trade, and 'to promote the trade of England'. A prohibitive duty was imposed on Irish wool exports, with the result that 40,000 Irish workers (for the most part from the English colonial population) became unemployed. By 1822, wool manufacturing had dwindled to 50 per cent of its original output, and although the Ulster linen and cotton industries, not being subject to the outrageous export taxes that applied to wool, thrived, many of the Protestant working population had been thrust into poverty and became more and more dependent on the potato for sustenance.

Although the Act of Union, which ostensibly united England, Scotland and Ireland, had come into effect in 1801, Ireland continued to be regarded by mainland Britain as a hostile territory, with a population that was inferior to that of England. Canon John O'Rourke asserted that it was the

> frequently avowed policy of England to keep Ireland poor, and therefore feeble, that she might be held the more securely. For that reason she was not treated as a portion of a united kingdom, but as an enemy who had become England's slave by conquest, who was her rival in manufactures of various kinds, who might undersell her in foreign markets, and, in fact, who might grow rich and powerful enough to assert her independence.

JOHN, LORD FITZGIBBON
Earl of Clare

O'Rourke's partisan view is reinforced by a statement of Lord Clare ('no friend to Ireland', according to the reverend canon) that

> The Parliament of England seem to have considered the permanent debility of Ireland as the best security of the British crown, and the Irish Parliament to have rested the security of the colony upon maintaining a perpetual and impossible barrier against the ancient inhabitants of this country.

Whatever the views of parliament, famine relief was forthcoming from private subscriptions and two government grants that were voted on in June and July 1822 – the government grants alone totalled £300,000, and were made in order to provide 'for the employment of the poor in Ireland, and other purposes relating thereto, as the exigency of affairs may require'. The London Tavern Committee raised subscriptions totalling just over £304,000, and the

Dublin Mansion House Committee raised a little over £30,000. About a million people required financial assistance during the crisis. All relief was administered centrally through Dublin Castle, the seat of the English administration in Ireland. The Dublin Castle committee distributed relief funds to local committees. A famine during 1816 and 1817 had given rise to the Poor Employment Act of 1817, which laid down provisions for a wide range of public works, including the building of roads, bridges and canals and many other projects, such as turf-cutting, that were regarded as being beneficial to the public. Those employed in the various schemes were remunerated with cash or with food.

Building new roads and repairing old ones was the most common type of public works initiative during the famine years. The scale of the public works projects was enormous. In July 1822 it was reported that in County Limerick alone, there were 'upwards of 10,000 persons at present employed', mostly on the building of roads. The work was not

DUBLIN CASTLE

only materially useful, but tended to improve the infrastructure. The 1823 report of a civil engineer, John Killaly, provides an insight into the road building works being carried out, their cost and the improved communications that they brought about:

> Feeling, therefore, that some new impulse and direction should be given to the pursuits of the peasantry in this district, with a view to

PHOTOGRAPH taken late 19th century of touring pleasure craft on a stretch of the Boyne Navigation, perhaps close to Rossnaree and Newgrange.

their moral and political improvement, I have taken the liberty of submitting my ideas as to the utility of the proposed canal, in addition to which I would beg leave respectfully to suggest the propriety of improving the roads at present nearly impassable, which run along the heads of the bays of Liscannor, Seafield, Dunbeg, and Kilkea, with the road from thence to the market town of Kilrush, and also that from Liscannor bay by Innistymond, to the town of Ennis. These works would not only afford extensive employment to the poor during the present season of calamity, but, when perfected, and that our fisheries are put upon the judicious footing which I trust ere long the Legislature will effect, would open a facile communication to good market towns for the produce of a trade, which should, in this part of Ireland, if reasonably well managed, be exceedingly lucrative. The expense attendant upon the execution of these works I estimate at about £4000.

ACCOUNTS and papers published in 1846, showing sums paid to John Killaly.

The increase in road building had a military benefit
as well – while working on a relief scheme in County
Clare Killaly wrote to William H. Gregory, the Under-
Secretary of Ireland, at his office in Dublin Castle, that
the road being constructed would 'tend materially
to civilise and bring under the control of the laws, a
population hitherto very untractable'. Another civil
engineer, Richard Griffiths, a supervisor of public works
schemes in Abbeyfeale, County Limerick, described
the area as a 'wild and uncultivated district which
has hitherto been a secure asylum for robbers and
murderers', and recommended that a bridge be built
over the River Alla at Freemount 'to enable the troops to
act on both sides of the river in times of flood'.

Despite the donation of seed potatoes and the
provision of public works schemes for the employment
of the distressed, government policies were such that
the invidious situation of the vast majority of the
residents of the island of Ireland remained unchanged
and the stage was set for an even greater disaster.

The Political and Social Background to the Great Famine

Property was regarded as having no duties attached to it. *Anthony Trollope*

To understand why the potato famine that began in the mid-1840s had such a devastating effect, it is helpful to have an understanding of the political and social structure prevailing in Ireland at the time.

The last quarter of the 18th century had ushered in an unexpected period of hope and optimism for the Catholics of Ireland. At that time, most of the wealth, property and political power were in the hands of a small percentage of the population, the Anglo-Protestant ascendancy. This minority population was descended from British settlers who had been given large estates in Ireland and, in return, were charged with keeping the local population under control and preventing rebellion against the crown. Successive laws, later referred to collectively as the Penal Laws, had gradually eroded the rights of Catholics to land ownership and education. At a time when the vote was open only to landowners, these harsh laws had the effect of disenfranchising large swaths of the population.

Under the occupying administration Ireland had little legislative freedom. Although there was an Irish parliament in Dublin, all the legislation emanating from it had to be ratified by the parliament at Westminster. Thus the legislative agenda was controlled by Westminster, as was all Irish trade, and punitive export duties were applied to Irish goods to ensure that they didn't compete unfavourably with English goods. The need for reform had become apparent to an unlikely group – the Protestant ascendancy itself. While most opposed the idea of Catholic emancipation, concerned that the island would gain independence of England, there was a group of Anglo-Protestants who espoused and campaigned for the right of Catholics to equality under the law.

HENRY GRATTAN
– although loyal to Britain he was in favour of Catholic emancipation and wanted to reform the Irish parliament to allow it to make laws independently.

One such campaigner, Trinity-educated Henry Grattan, was elected to the Dublin parliament in 1775. In 1782 he introduced a constitution that lifted many of the legislative restrictions that had been imposed on the parliament. He delivered a rousing speech to the unshackled legislature.

> I found Ireland on her knees, I watched over her with a paternal solicitude; I have traced her progress from injuries to arms, and from arms to liberty … Ireland is now a nation … no longer a wretched colony, returning thanks to her governor for his rapine, and to her king for his oppression …

The parliament became known as Grattan's Parliament. The legislative freedom it conferred was to be short-lived.

Although Grattan wanted to achieve Catholic emancipation through peaceful means, there were those who wanted to break Ireland's connection with Britain completely. In 1791, encouraged by the revolutions in France and America, a young Protestant lawyer, Theobald Wolfe Tone, founded the Society of United Irishmen. Initially he conceived it as a campaign group with the aim of severing the country's connection with England, which he derided as the 'never-failing source of all our political evils'. The peaceful principles

'IRISH GRATITUDE'
satrical cartoon featuiring Henry Flood, Henry Grattan, Edmond Sexton Viscount Pery. By James Gillray, published 1782

of the organisation had soon been replaced by the aim of full independence through whatever means necessary, including armed rebellion.

In 1793, fearful of the unrest in revolutionary France, Westminster passed the Catholic Relief Act, which extended the franchise to three million Irish Catholics. Despite having finally achieved the vote, the newly enfranchised Catholics tended to vote with their landlords, who encouraged them by granting them leases, 'forty-shilling freeholds', on small plots of land, just large enough to accommodate a small cabin, with a bit of land for growing potatoes for food, and grain with which to pay the rent.

WOLFE TONE
depicted on a silk
cigarette card

Despite the concessions introduced by the 1793 legislation, Wolfe Tone was determined on violent uprising as a means of achieving full independence for the country. He enlisted the support of France, and although an attempt to land a French expeditionary force at Bantry Bay in 1796 had to be aborted, Wolfe Tone continued to plot a nationwide uprising. In May 1798 plans for the Dublin uprising were betrayed by a spy and it failed before it had even started. However, risings took place around the country, although they were quickly crushed, except in Wexford, where the rebels held out for several weeks before being defeated. Wolfe Tone was captured on a French vessel, the *Hoche*. He was brought to Dublin, where he was tried and sentenced to death. Although he asked to be executed by firing squad, claiming that right as a military prisoner in time of war, he was sentenced to be hanged. He cut his own throat on the eve of his planned execution.

After the failure of the 1798 rebellion, it was clear that an

CHARLES CORNWALLIS, 1st Marquess Cornwallis, by Thomas Gainsborough, 1783

increasingly nervous Britain would not allow Grattan's Parliament to retain the modicum of independence it had achieved. The loss of the American colony focused the prime minister, William Pitt, on the necessity of strengthening the ties between Britain and Ireland. Lord Cornwallis, who had led the British army to victory in the rebellion, was made Lord Lieutenant of Ireland, tasked with guiding an Act of Union (for the unification of Britain and Ireland) through the Irish parliament. A similar Act was debated in the Westminster parliament.

Cornwallis had an unenviable task. The initial proposals were heavily opposed and the Lord Lieutenant had to go on an offensive in order to shepherd through the legislation. Numerous new Irish peerages were created and Catholics were assuaged with the promise that emancipation, without which no Catholic could be elected to parliament, would be a priority. In March 1800, the Act was passed. The Irish parliament was abolished

WILLIAM PITT THE YOUNGER (1759–1806), detail, by John Hoppner (1758–1810)

and the Kingdom of Ireland became part of the United Kingdom of Great Britain and Ireland, with effect from 1 January 1801. Prime Minister Pitt had every intention of honouring the promise of Catholic emancipation, but the king, George III, refused to support him in this and Pitt resigned from office.

The failure of the 1798 rebellion and the subsequent enactment of the Act of Union inspired Robert Emmet, the son of a doctor and a student at Trinity College Dublin, to breathe new life into the United Irishmen and plot a new uprising. His rebellion, poorly planned and badly executed, was a failure from the beginning. Fewer than 100 of the expected 2,000 rebels turned up in Dublin on the appointed day in July 1803, and the rebellion turned into little more than a drunken brawl, during the course of which a Dublin judge was pulled from his carriage and murdered. Emmet went into hiding, but was captured, tried for treason and hanged. Despite the dismal failure of his

ROBERT EMMET
watercolour on ivory, miniature portrait by John Comerford.

rebellion, Emmet entered the annals of Irish political martyrs, not least for his stirring speech from the dock after he was condemned.

DANIEL O'CONNELL
lithograph by Hoffy, 1847

With stronger ties to Britain than had ever existed before and with full Catholic emancipation off the negotiating table, Ireland seemed to be moving backwards politically. In 1811, an Irish Catholic lawyer, Daniel O'Connell, appalled by the senseless violence of the 1798 and 1803 rebellions, founded the Catholic Board to campaign for Catholic emancipation (the right to sit in parliament). In 1823 he established the Catholic Association, which campaigned for broader change, in areas such as tenants' rights and economic development. The annual subscription of a shilling was used to fund the campaign for Catholic emancipation.

As a result of the campaign, although King George IV had inherited the vehement opposition to the idea from his father, King George III, the official line began to soften. After several years O'Connell

decided the time was right to take things a step further and in 1828 he stood as a parliamentary candidate in a by-election in County Clare. He won the election, but was unable to take his seat because the Oath of Supremacy instituted in the 16th century by King Henry VIII and required of all MPs was incompatible with Catholicism. Home Secretary Robert Peel realised that preventing O'Connell taking his seat would lead to more unrest and violence in Ireland. A reading of the mood of the English public showed that there was also much sympathy there for the Catholic cause, so Prime Minister Arthur Wellesley, the Dublin-born Duke of Wellington, worked with Peel to establish the right of all Christians to sit in Parliament. The Roman Catholic Relief Act became law in 1829, but the legislation was not applied retrospectively and O'Connell had to stand for election again. He took his seat in February 1830. The 1829 Act was a double-edged sword – while it gave Catholics the right to sit in the parliament at Westminster, it increased the property qualification for voters to five times its original value, effectively disenfranchising most Irish Catholics. The Reform Act of 1832 disqualified all but one voter in every 83 who had previously been entitled to vote.

Having achieved Catholic emancipation, O'Connell – who was now hailed in Ireland as 'Liberator' – turned his efforts to the repeal of the Act of Union. In 1830 he founded the Repeal Association, which had the aim of separating the two kingdoms, with Queen Victoria continuing as Queen of Ireland. The drive for separation became known as 'repeal' and the movement had appeal across the board – the middle classes took a pragmatic view, seeing it as a way of gaining control of the day-to-day administration of the country, while the Catholic lower classes regarded it as a means of achieving their long-denied nationhood after centuries of being sidelined.

O'Connell's hugely successful strategy of holding 'monster' meetings around the country to promote

DETAIL OF SIR ROBERT PEEL, 2nd Bt, by Henry William Pickersgill (1782–1875)

repeal for Ireland enraged Prime Minister Peel, who was vehemently opposed to the idea. In late 1843 the government banned a monster meeting planned for Clontarf, outside Dublin, and O'Connell was later arrested, together with some other leaders of the movement, and charged with conspiracy. His conviction carried a sentence of a £2,000 fine and one year's imprisonment, although he served only a quarter of that, and was released early when his conviction was quashed by the House of Lords, who recognised the affair as the malicious prosecution that it was. However, Peel had succeeded in removing O'Connell from the political circuit – albeit very briefly – and without his leadership, the Repeal Association began to splinter. The focus shifted to the Young Ireland movement, founded in 1842 by William Smith O'Brien, who rejected O'Connell's

WILLIAM SMITH O'BRIEN

engagement with establishment politics, and saw armed insurrection as the way forward.

Against the backdrop of the machinations of the political classes, the poor people of Ireland were living in conditions that had reached a nadir of wretchedness. Almost half the population were living in dwellings that were graded as the fourth and lowest classification in the population census of 1841 – 'windowless mud cabins of a single room'. An 1837 survey of an area in Donegal with a population of 9,000 found that 'furniture was a real luxury in most houses, as among those 9,000 people were only 10 beds, 93 chairs, 243 stools'. A Royal Commission Report of 1843 into the living conditions of the poor stated that most of the misery came about as a direct result of landlord absenteeism. Irish tenants paid, on average, 70 per cent more than their counterparts in England. The payment of these 'rack' rents meant that people had barely enough left to feed themselves. The plots of land they farmed were just large enough for subsistence. Since 1704

POVERTY in rural Ireland, 1840s.

DIGGING FOR POTATOES
contemporary engraving

the Penal Laws had required all land owned by Catholics to be divided between all the descendants, legitimate and illegitimate, of a landowner – by the 1840s subdivision after subdivision had produced a preponderance of tiny plots of land. Most of the land was farmed by the tenant farmers who made up the bulk of the rural population. Tenants had no security of tenure, being subject to eviction at the whim of their landlord or his agent. Absenteeism allowed landlords to enjoy all of the rights and privileges of land ownership, while paying lip service, at best, to the duties and responsibilities they owed their tenants.

In 1841, the English novelist Anthony Trollope, while working at the General Post Office in London, applied for and was appointed to the position of postal surveyor's clerk in Ireland. He was charged with making inspections of the postal service in Connacht. While he provided his employers with a good account of the day-to-day workings of the service, he also observed the conditions of people living in that part of the country. His analysis of the causes of the situation of the poor was timely, and he laid the blame squarely at the door of the landowners, both Protestant and Catholic, for their greed and their shirking of their responsibilities.

ANTHONY TROLLOPE
undated photograph

> The fault had been the lowness of education and consequent want of principle among the middle classes; and this fault had been found as strongly marked among the Protestants as it had been among the Roman Catholics. Young men were brought up to do nothing. Property was regarded as having no duties attached to it. Men became rapacious, and determined to extract the uttermost farthing out of the land within their power, let the consequences to the people on that land be what they might.

His view of the system of tenant farming as it was set up in the country was that it was 'the scourge of Ireland'.

Men there held tracts of ground, very often at their full value, paying for them such proportion of rent as a farmer could afford to pay in England and live. But the Irish tenant would by no means consent to be a farmer. It was needful to him that he should be a gentleman, and that his sons should be taught to live and amuse themselves as the sons of gentlemen – barring any such small trifle as education. They did live in this way; and to enable them to do so, they underlet their land in small patches, and at an amount of rent to collect which took the whole labour of their tenants, and the whole produce of the small patch, over and above the quantity of potatoes absolutely necessary to keep that tenant's body and soul together.

And thus a state of things was engendered in Ireland which discouraged labour, which discouraged improvements in farming, which discouraged any produce from the land except the potato crop; which maintained one class of men in what they considered to be the gentility of idleness, and another class, the people of the country, in the abjectness of poverty.

These abjectly poor people, a third of whom were almost wholly dependent on the potato for sustenance, were poised for a disaster not of their making. The introduction of a new hardy breed of potato, the Lumper, in the early years of the 19th century, had made potato eating popular throughout the country. Requiring little fertiliser and capable of surviving in poor soil, the Lumper became the potato of choice for subsistence farmers. In 1700 it was estimated that a farmer in Connacht would have eaten one meal of potatoes each day. By 1800, a farmer in that part of the country was consuming two meals of potatoes daily. By 1840, this had increased to three meals,

GATHERING POTATOES
contemporary engraving

with a total daily consumption of 5–6 kilos (12–14 lb) per adult male.

Although cheap and abundant the potato had a relatively short storage time of 9 months – unlike grain it could not be stored against hard times and had to be planted every year in order to produce an annual crop.

A potato blight struck in 1845 and after several months it became clear that it was going to take longer than a year to resolve the situation. The British government has, rightly, been criticised for its inadequate response to the crisis. However, Irish MPs constituted about 20 per cent of the Westminster parliament. Why did they do so little to alleviate the suffering of the people of Ireland? Most were Protestant, and because of the hefty property qualification for eligibility for election, they all came from the upper echelons of Irish society. The devastation caused by famine was happening in the countryside, at a remove from their lives, which proceeded as normal during the famine years. Many Irish MPs were also landlords and were fearful of having to assume the responsibility under the Poor Law of sustaining their tenants until the situation returned to normal. In most cases they campaigned for more government aid purely so that their tenants would not become a drain on their finances.

Irish politics was factional, with different party groupings agitating for important rights such as free tenure, or 'tenant right' (the right of the tenant to be paid, on leaving a tenancy, by his successor in

FREE TRADE
contemporary
satirical engraving.

CONFIDENCE   AND   DIFFIDENCE.

the tenancy). These rights were almost completely irrelevant to the bulk of the people affected by the famine. They were the poorest of the poor – cottiers, smallholders and labourers, most of them sub-tenants who would gain nothing from improvements in the tenancy laws. So, while MPs railed against the egregiousness of absentee Irish landlords, they were not in the vanguard of those protesting for employment and affordable food during the harsh years when the potato blight introduced the very real spectre of starvation. Landholders determined the politics of the day while the poor starved.

The detachment of politicians from the real world of those afflicted by famine is illustrated by an instruction issued by William Smith O'Brien of the Young Ireland movement, who attempted to raise an insurrection in 1848, while famine stalked the land. When crowds answered his call to rise against the government, he told them to go home and come back with enough food to sustain them for four days.

WILLIAM SMITH O'BRIEN mustering men at Mullinahone, County Tipperary, during the Rebellion of 1848

Phytophthora Infestans Arrives in Ireland

One family in twenty of the people will not have a single potato left on Christmas Day next.
Very Reverend McEvoy, Parish Priest of Kells, County Meath

In early September 1845 the potatoes that were being sold in the London markets were found to be unfit for human consumption. To outward appearances they were normal, but when they were boiled and cut open they revealed slimy, brownish-black flesh. Growers were soon doing spot checks on their potato fields and speculation as to the cause of the disease was rife. It was generally agreed that some sort of fungus was responsible. One observer reported that '[I]t first appears as a bluish speck on the potato and then spreads rapidly.' Another account described the disease as 'beginning with a damp spot on some part of the potato'.

A similar potato disease was first noticed in Ireland in the middle of September, moving rapidly from the coast of Wexford throughout the entire island, appearing in different places at different times. Theories abounded as to how it had reached Ireland: it had travelled in the holds of ships bound for England from North America; it first appeared in Germany in 1842, then travelled to Belgium where it was particularly virulent in Liège; it was in Canada in 1844 and spread throughout the United Kingdom in 1845.

POTATO with blight

People in Ireland provided more fanciful reasons: the static electricity caused by the recently introduced steam locomotives; volcanic vapours from the middle of the Earth drifting over Ireland; a divine punishment for the sins of the people.

Sir James Murray, MD, attributed the blight to electricity.

> During the last season, the clouds were charged with excessive electricity; and yet there was little

or no thunder to draw off that excess from the atmosphere. In the damp and variable autumn this surcharge of electrical matter was attracted by the moist, succulent, and pointed leaves of the potatoes.

It wasn't until much later that the cause of the potato blight was identified as Phythopthora infestans (an oomycete rather than a fungus), now known to cause so-called late blight in the potato and its family members, the tomato and aubergine.

Whatever the source of the disease, its effects were devastating. In Ireland the blight manifested itself on the potato plant leaves as brown spots of different shapes and sizes. The leaves then turned black and curled up, and then they began to rot. The rot spread throughout the plant and a dreadful stench became noticeable – it was reported from County Meath that 'the labourers were obliged to give up digging from the disagreeable smell'. When the potatoes were dug up they looked whole and

INTERIOR OF A FISHERMAN'S COTTAGE, Galway, by Alfred Downing Fripp, 1822–1895

edible, but contact with the air caused them to shrivel
and blacken within several days. Early observations
showed that initial infestation seemed to have a

random and haphazard pattern. Sometimes the blight was confined to the potatoes planted beside hedges or under trees, and sometimes one part of a field was affected while the remainder was blight free. The contemporary chronicler of the Great Famine, Canon John O'Rourke, said that he sometimes observed 'the very first symptoms of the disease opposite an open gateway, as if a blighting wind had rushed in, making for some distance a sort of avenue of discoloured leaves and stalks, about the width of a gateway at first, but becoming wider onwards'.

The parish priest of Kells, County Meath, Reverend McEvoy, sent this report in October 1845, during the early days of the first manifestation of the blight:

A FAMILY struggles to find potatoes that are not affected by blight.

> On my most minute personal inspection of the state of the potato crop in this most fertile potato-growing locale, is founded my inexpressibly painful conviction, that one family in twenty of the people will not have a single potato left on Christmas day next.

Soon after the appearance of the blight the government charged the Royal Irish Constabulary with appointing inspectors to travel around the country and submit reports on the state of affairs in each county. As the weeks wore on, the accounts they provided became less positive and even the language of the reports became sparse and devoid of embellishment.

Initial accounts from different parts of the country were favourable, giving rise to the belief that the infestation was partial and had, in some cases, been arrested. On 1 October it was reported from Cork that the situation was '[M]ost cheering on the whole, notwithstanding very partial failures … On the whole the crop appears above average. The failures are of a very limited extent.' In Galway it was predicted that '[A]n abundant crop is expected: more so in some districts than the oldest inhabitant can remember.' The report from Clare stated categorically that there would be 'no loss either from failure or disease in the early crop to reduce it below

average. From all appearances the late crop will be
unusually abundant …'. In Donegal the crop was
'apparently healthy and fruitful; possibly some to
spare.' It looked as if it might even be a bumper year
for the potato crop.

Less than three weeks later the accounts were
becoming more alarming. A report from Westmeath

SCENE IN LEINSTER
1840s, from *The
Illustrated London
News*.

on 17 October said that scarcely a potato had been untouched by the disease, and in Meath the failure was described as 'very general'. In Ballinahinch in County Down about a quarter of the crop was destroyed, although 'for upwards of a week, however, the disease has made no progress'. Downpatrick was faring less well, with a third of the crop destroyed. The crop in Kilkenny was 'more or less diseased throughout the district'.

On 21 October the situation in Wexford was that '[I]n some places, the root has altogether disappeared, having melted into the earth, leaving the withered stalk behind. Everyone is selling off as fast as possible at low rates.' In East Galway 'the poor people who rented the fields said they were not worth digging'. In Navan, County Meath, 'complaints of general failure are numerous. In many instances more than one third destroyed. Very few fields free from disease. Only two or three farmers have commenced to dig out their crop, most persons being of opinion that the longer they remain in the ground the less they are damaged.'

In the third week of October the Royal Agricultural Improvement Society of Ireland appointed a special committee to prepare a report on the subject of the failure of the potato crop. A meeting was convened on 28 October, chaired by the Lord Mayor of Dublin, John L. Arabin. The town clerk had sent a report to the committee on foot of a recent inspection of the potatoes dug from

DESTITUTION 1840s from *The Pictorial Times.*

eight or 10 acres that had been stored in a sound state three weeks previously. He reported that it was now difficult to find a sound potato amongst them. The committee found it 'advisable that the Council should now direct the attention of the Irish Government to the now undoubted fact, that a great portion of the potato crop in this country was affected by the disease in question.'

By mid-November it was apparent that that year's potato crop had failed nationwide, and that for the first time in recorded history a serious crop failure was affecting the entire country, yet no measures were put in place to prevent wholesale starvation. Some social reformers even considered the blight to be a blessing that would end an almost total dependence on the potato, ignoring the reasons for the existence of that dependence. While people faced into a winter of starvation, the grain harvest was being exported from the country. At the end of October Fr McEvoy of Kells noted that

SEARCHING
for potatoes in a stubble field

[W]ith starvation at our doors, grimly staring us, vessels laden with our whole hope of existence, our provisions, are hourly wafted from our every port. From one milling establishment I have last night seen no less that fifty dray-loads of meal moving on to Drogheda, thence to go to feed the foreigner, leaving starvation and death the soon and certain fate of the toil and sweat that raised this food.

THE LORD LIEUTENANT of Ireland, Lord Heytesbury

The Mansion House Committee in Dublin sent a delegation, which included Daniel O'Connell, the Duke of Leinster and Henry Grattan, to the Lord Lieutenant of Ireland, Lord Heytesbury, with a resolution passed by the committee:

… we have ascertained beyond the shadow of a doubt, that considerably more than one-third of the entire potato crop in Ireland has been already destroyed by the potato disease; and that such disease has not, by any means, ceased its ravages, but, on the contrary, it is daily extending more and more; and that no reasonable conjecture can be formed with respect to the limits of its effects, short of the

ATTACK ON A potato store. Engraving from *The Illustrated London News*, 1842

> destruction of the entire remaining potato crop … We are
> thus unfortunately able to proclaim … that in Ireland famine
> of a most hideous description must be immediate and
> pressing, and that pestilence of the most frightening kind is
> certain and not remote, unless immediately prevented …

The resolution was an urgent call to the British government to open Irish ports to food imports and to halt the exportation of Irish grain. When the resolution was submitted the quantity of oats that had already been exported 'was nearly adequate to feed the entire people of Ireland, and to avert the now certain famine'. Other resolutions asked for the immediate employment of people on public works and a ban on the use of grain for brewing and distilling.

Lord Heytesbury's reply to the committee made it clear that there would be no speedy government intervention to alleviate the starvation that was the inevitable outcome of the blight. He gave various reasons: Scientists had been sent from England to investigate the nature of the blight afflicting the potato crop but had yet to make a definitive report; reports from magistrates on the progress of the potato harvest were contradictory; a decision on the proper measures to be taken would be premature. He concluded:

THE FREEMAN'S JOURNAL was the oldest nationalist newspaper in Ireland. It was founded in 1763 by Charles Lucas

There is no immediate pressure in the market … your suggestions … require to be maturely weighed before they can be adopted.

News of the Lord Lieutenant's response soon spread – the *Freeman's Journal* was scathing:

They may starve! Such in spirit, if not in words, was the reply given yesterday by the English Viceroy, to the memorial of the deputation, which, in the name of the Lords and Commons of Ireland, prayed that the food of this kingdom be preserved, lest the people thereof perish.

The only assistance offered to an increasingly despairing population was advice on how to cook the diseased potatoes, much of which involved cutting out the inedible parts of the potatoes and cooking the unaffected flesh with cabbage, salted herrings, salted butter, salted pork, lard and bacon and boiled rice. How the small quantity of potato flesh salvaged could replace the usual quantity of potatoes consumed by those who were completely dependent on them was not described. At the time, adult males consumed in the region of 6 kg (14 lbs) of potatoes each day; adult females and 11–15-year-olds 5 kg (11 lbs); younger children 2.2 kg (5 lbs). Any potatoes that survived the blight would clearly not be sufficient to feed the population that was dependent on them.

On 15 November the scientific commission appointed by the government reported to the prime minister, Sir Robert Peel, on the state of the Irish potato crop.

SATIRICAL illustration of Sir Robert Peel in *Punch*, 1845

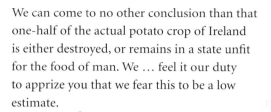

We can come to no other conclusion than that one-half of the actual potato crop of Ireland is either destroyed, or remains in a state unfit for the food of man. We ... feel it our duty to apprize you that we fear this to be a low estimate.

This meant that the blight had reduced the value of the potato crop in 1845 from £18 million to £9 million. Peel was alarmed by the report, although he wrote to the Lord Lieutenant of the 'tendency in Ireland to disregard accuracy and to exaggerate'. Lord Heytesbury reassured him that

Even if the crops turned out to be as bad as is now apprehended ... [T]here will be enough saved for immediate consumption ... Gloomy as all this is, it would hardly be prudent to adopt any very strong or decisive measures till the final result of the potato

BRIDGET O'DONNELL and her children.

harvest can be fully ascertained. The digging
will not be over till about the second week in
November.

Despite Peel's reservations as to the veracity of
the reports coming from Ireland, the government
appointed a commission to enquire into the
situation. The Lord Mayor of Dublin was
interviewed by a member of the commission, who
assured him that the government was fully prepared
to take such steps as 'might be found necessary for
the protection of the people', when the emergency
should arise. 'Many people thought it had arisen
already,' declared Canon O'Rourke. 'And on they
went enquiring when they should have been acting.'

In fact, the government was acting to provide
famine relief in the short term. Robert Peel had
campaigned for several years for the repeal of the
Corn Laws, a body of protectionist legislation
enacted in 1815 that provided for heavy duties
on imported grain, allowing British grain to

PORTRAIT of
Sir Robert Peel,
2nd Baronet
(1788–1850)

be sold at inflated prices without any competition from cheaper imported grain. The Anti-Corn Law League was established in 1838 in industrial Manchester to agitate for the repeal of the Corn Laws, which maintained artificially high prices for British grain during a period when factory owners were trying to reduce the wages of their workers. This pitched landowners against manufacturers and Peel had taken some time to be persuaded of the merits of the League's case for repeal. A consummate politician, he eventually declared his hand when he saw how the winds of public opinion were blowing. He used the example of the failure of the Irish potato crop as an object illustration of how the Corn Laws were preventing the importation of food to feed a starving nation.

On 15 October 1845 he wrote to the Lord Lieutenant of Ireland:

> The Accounts from Ireland of the potato crop … are very alarming … the remedy is the removal of all impediments to the import of all kinds of human food … to remit the duty on Indian corn expressly for the purpose of averting famine would make it very invidious to retain a duty on other species of corn more generally applicable to the food of man … Who will re-establish

the Corn Laws once abrogated,
though from a casual and temporary
pressure?

In November 1845 Peel established a Relief
Commission to organise the setting up of food
depots around Ireland – the price of food had risen
sharply to the point where many could not afford
to buy it. By the following summer 600 depots had
been established. In contravention of the Corn

THE CENTRAL SOUP
Depot, Barrack
Street, Cork

Laws he secretly ordered a load of Indian cornmeal (a species of corn not 'generally applicable to the food of man') to a value of £100,000, to be shipped from America to Ireland and sold cheaply to famine relief committees in an effort to stem rising food prices. Despite his efforts, the Indian corn was not

THE MACEDONIAN
US Frigate, laden with provisions for the destitute Irish

successful, leading as it did to serious digestive problems in people who were already starving – the meal comprised sharp fragments of corn and required very long cooking. People were used to softer grains that required little cooking and the corn, essentially roughage, passed through their digestive systems too quickly, causing severe diarrhoea without providing adequate nutrition. Instructions as to the proper cooking of the meal were not forthcoming until early 1847.

In February 1846, in an attempt to persuade the House of Commons to pass legislation for the repeal of the Corn Laws, Peel drew on the sufferings of the people of Ireland.

> When you are exhorting a suffering people to fortitude under their privations, when you are telling them, 'these are the chastenings of an all-wise and merciful Providence, sent for some inscrutable but just and beneficent purpose … when you are thus addressing your suffering fellow subjects … may God grant that by your decision of this night you may have laid in store for yourselves the consolation of reflecting that such calamities are, in truth, the dispensations of Providence – that they have not been caused, they have not been

ENGRAVING of
Daniel O'Connell

aggravated by laws of man restricting, in the hour of scarcity, the supply of food!

The Corn Laws were finally repealed in 1846 with the parliamentary support of Daniel O'Connell's Repeal Party. By then, however, there were food shortages all over Europe, with little grain available for importation, and the repeal of the legislation came too late to have any impact on the availability of corn in Ireland. Although he had supported the prime minister on the question of the Corn Laws, O'Connell loathed Peel personally, and despite the prime minister's well-intentioned and sometimes successful famine relief measures the Repeal Party joined with Liberals and Tory rebels to bring down Peel's Conservative government in June of that year.

The Liberal (or Whig) party was now in power, and the new prime minister was Lord John Russell. Based on previous experience of famine in

Ireland, Russell expected that the emergency situation would last no longer than a year. Although, like Peel, the new prime minister was quite sympathetic towards Ireland and her people, a large faction in his government believed that state intervention in the form of famine relief would encourage idleness and lack of self-reliance. From the Victorian establishment perspective, Irish peasants quite readily came under the heading of 'the undeserving poor'.

JOHN RUSSELL, 1st Earl Russell, by Sir Francis Grant

Early Responses to the Crisis

It forms no part of the functions of government to provide supplies of food or to increase the productive powers of the land.

Sir Charles Trevelyan, Assistant Secretary to the Treasury

One of Peel's initiatives for famine relief was the introduction of a Public Works Act, which was passed in March 1846. It established a mechanism whereby people would be provided with employment under the aegis of the Board of Works, a body established in 1831 to provide employment on public works schemes aimed at alleviating the effects of earlier famines. A Drainage Bill and a Fisheries Bill were also introduced – it was anticipated that loans would be forthcoming under both schemes that would have the dual benefit of improving river drainages and facilitating the construction of small harbours and piers, while at the same time providing necessary employment for those affected by the potato blight. The *Downpatrick Recorder* of 7 February 1846 described the various bills as

> … so many steps in the right direction. They will tend to the improvement of the physical condition of the country. Such measures ought to stop the mouths of agitators; and the peasantry of Ireland are not so devoid of discrimination as not to perceive the difference between an English government which takes means to feed and clothe them, and those who despoil them of their hard-earned pence and shillings.

IGHTERCOA, County Kerry. A cottage, described as 'giving the impression of dirty cow houses, whilst the land around .. ... in a poor state of cultivation.'

Late in spring 1846 work commenced on drainage schemes and

SKETCH BY JAMES MAHONY on the road, at Cahera, of a famished boy and girl turning up the ground looking for potatoes

on the building of the so-called 'famine roads' (roads that were built for no purpose and that led nowhere). Those wishing to be employed through the scheme had to apply to their local relief committees for 'relief tickets'. In order to qualify they had to show themselves to be 'persons who are destitute of means of support, or for whose support such employment is actually necessary'. The work was back-breaking and the people who worked on the public works projects (women and children included) were weakened by hunger. Some dropped dead where they worked – those who survived the rigours of the labour were paid badly and irregularly. Bartering rather than buying and selling was the traditional means of exchange among the poorer classes, and many people were ill-equipped for the financial transactions involved in buying food.

By now, potatoes were selling for five pence per stone (the daily potato ration for an adult male) and a day's wages was eight pence. People needed more than work – they also needed to be protected against rising food prices. In September 1846 it was noted that the price of oats had increased to the point where the poor could no longer afford to buy the grain. Depots for the sale of Indian cornmeal were set up, but they were badly staffed and the opening hours were inadequate to the task of distributing food to the lines of people queuing up in hope of sustenance.

The Liberal government had given responsibility for the administration of famine relief measures to Sir Charles Trevelyan, Assistant Secretary to the Treasury, an able administrator who had acquitted himself well in India and in the field of education. His was a disastrous appointment for Ireland. He was a micro manager, working into the small hours of the morning on the minutiae of the documents that crossed his desk. He believed that the famine in Ireland was the will of an 'all wise Providence', a 'mechanism for reducing surplus population', and his laissez-

SIR CHARLES TREVELYAN,
Assistant Secretary to the Treasury

faire approach to famine relief reflected the current thinking of the Liberal party. He believed that

> … [T]he judgement of God sent the calamity the teach the Irish a lesson, that calamity must not be too much mitigated … The real evil with which we have to contend is not the physical evil of the Famine, but the moral evil of the selfish, perverse and turbulent character of the people.

SIR CHARLES TREVELYAN, detail from a group photograph

Trevelyan blocked the importation of Indian cornmeal destined for the relief of the starving poor because he didn't want people to become habitually dependent on the government for handouts. He defended the export of Irish-grown grain during the famine years in the interests of free trade. He was suspicious (as were many in the government) of the efficacy of the public works schemes and their susceptibility to being abused. As people died of hunger and overwork he wrote to the Under-

Secretary, Richard Pennefather, at Dublin Castle:

> I am commanded … to state that, having reason to believe that numerous persons who do not really stand in need of relief are employed on the works … and the rates of wages are given exceeding what is required for providing subsistence for the workpeople and their families, and holding out a temptation to engage in the works carried on [under the legislation] in preference to other means of employment which are open to them, their Lordships request that you will suggest to the Lord Lieutenant that the Board of Works and the Relief commission should be directed to issue such instructions to the superintendents of the works and to the local relief committees, as will secure a due observance of the funds provided for the relief of the people suffering from the late failure of the potato crop in Ireland.

RENT ABATEMENT notice in 1846 from the Earl of Charlemont to his tenants in Counties Armagh and Tyrone

FAMINE meal ticket

In October 1846 Trevelyan wrote to Lord Monteagle, who had large estates in County Limerick:

… the ability of even the most powerful government is extremely limited in dealing with a social evil of this description. It forms no part of the functions of government to provide supplies of food or to increase the productive powers of the land. In the great institution of the business of society, it falls to the share of government to protect the merchant and the agriculturalist in the free exercise of their respective employments, but not itself to carry on those employments; and the condition of a community depends upon the result of the efforts which each member of it makes in his private and individual capacity …

Trevelyan was immortalised as Sir Gregory Hardlines in one of Anthony Trollope's 'Irish' novels, *The Three Clerks*, and, more famously, in the mournful ballad 'The Fields of Athenry',

LORD MONTEAGLE
1873 engraving

which tells of a young man sentenced to transportation for stealing food for his family from a shipment destined for export:

> By a lonely prison wall,
> I heard a young girl calling,
> Michael, they are taking you away.
> For you stole Trevelyan's corn,
> That the young might see the morn.
> Now a prison ship lies waiting in the bay.

MISERABLE conditions in Scalpeen, Limerick

Government initiatives for famine relief were still seen to be a purely temporary measure that could be withdrawn when the situation normalised. It was not anticipated that there would be a repeat of the blighted crop of 1845 and at the beginning of 1846 the signs and portents for a healthy potato crop that year were good. However, the initially healthy appearance of the year's potato crop was misleading. The seed potatoes that had been planted were of poor

FOOD RIOT in
Dungarvan
Pictorial Times, 1846

quality and the spring weather remained cool and damp, providing ideal conditions for the infecting spores of Phythopthora infestans to spread.

The blight travelled rapidly across the entire island that year, destroying almost every potato in the country. Canon O'Rourke reported that 'the potatoes never came to any maturity at all, and any that were thought worth the labour of digging, were hurried to market, and sold for any price they fetched, before they would melt away in the owners' hands.' A priest in Galway described the situation in his area: 'As to the potatoes, they are gone – clean gone. If travelling by night, you would know when a potato field was near by the smell. The fields present a space of withered black stalks.'

With the harvest that year producing sufficient potatoes to last only a month, panic began to set in. Despite the shortage of food, the grain exports continued. The public works schemes were intended to be wound up in August 1846, when the potato harvest was anticipated

to be in, but it had to be extended. However, now it was expected that the schemes would be financed locally, rather than receiving government funding, so a tax on local landowners would have to be raised. People were reported to be living on cabbage leaves and blackberries. Any available potatoes were unsound and caused bowel problems, including diarrhoea and dysentery. The government asked local constabularies to submit reports on the state of affairs in their districts, based on a series of specific questions. In County Waterford the Dungarvan constabulary submitted these responses:

Q. Is the acreage of potatoes planted in 1846
the same as the previous year?
A. One quarter less.
Q. What proportion of the 1846 crop is affected
by the blight?
A. All.
Q. Is the early or late crop affected?
A. Both.
Q. Is the surviving crop fit for food?
A. Very little of it.

OLD CHAPEL ROAD
Dungarvan, scene of
food riots

On 28 September 5,000 people protested in Dungarvan against the price of corn and its export and demanded that employment be offered on public works schemes. A mob tried to gain entry to the grain stores on the quay. The ringleaders, including Patrick Power of Killongford, were arrested and imprisoned. Later that day, when the crowd's demand for the release of the prisoners was refused, they looted several bakeries in the town for bread.

The military were called in and troops chased the crowd through the town. Stones were thrown at the soldiers and the Riot Act was read when the

THE MALL AND MALL-HOUSE, Youghal, County Cork, scene of food riots

crowd refused to disperse. Twenty-six shots were fired into the crowd and an innocent bystander later died of wounds received. All those arrested were later released, except for Patrick Power, identified as the ringleader, who was sentenced to a year's imprisonment with hard labour. Troops were sent to the town to maintain order while the grain ships were loaded, but the dock workers refused to load the cargo for fear of reprisals.

On 7 October, in Strancally, near Youghal in County Cork a large crowd tried to prevent a shipment of corn proceeding down the river Blackwater to Youghal. A local landlord defended the crowd's actions, viewing them as born of the starvation they were enduring. In some areas horses carrying corn were shot to prevent their loads being delivered.

The *Illustrated London News* reported sympathetically on the riots on 7 November.

> The distress, both in Youghal [County Cork] and Dungarvan, is truly appalling in the streets; for, without entering the houses, the miserable spectacle of haggard looks, crouching attitudes, sunken eyes and colourless lips and cheeks, unmistakably bespeaks the sufferings of the people.

Riots were taking place all around the country and the government mobilised 2,000 troops, organised into mobile columns, which could be sent where they were needed whenever trouble erupted. One starving resident of County Mayo remarked: 'Would to God the government would send us food instead of soldiers.'

By November the price of corn had trebled and people were reduced to foraging for wild berries, nettles, seaweed and limpets. They were even eating grass and weeds and drinking blood from live cattle. The threat of eviction loomed over many and tenants sold everything they had to avoid being turned out onto the roads. The winter of 1846–47 was the worst in living memory and the country was almost incessantly battered by bitter winds, snowstorms, sleet and hail. Houses disappeared under the snow. The dreadful weather persisted until April 1847. Fever, dysentery and typhoid found easy targets in those weakened by starvation. The *Cork Examiner* of 11 December 1846 described the ravages of fever:

> Out of one house in the Old Parish [of Dungarvan], three persons died in one fortnight – the father, the son and the mother, leaving after them six orphans who are also lying in fever.

A COMMUNITY of tenant farmers with their belongings being forcibly evicted from their homes.

HISTORIC MARKER
on the stone wall
of an old fever
hospital in Ireland,
built on the site of
a workhouse dating
back to the famine.

Another eyewitness account came from the resident magistrate of Cork, who visited Skibbereen.

I entered some of the hovels, and the scenes which presented themselves were such as no tongue or pen can convey the slightest idea of. In the first, six famished and ghastly skeletons, to all appearances dead, were huddled in a corner on some filthy straw, their sole covering what seemed a ragged horsecloth, their wretched legs hanging about, naked above the knees. I approached with horror, and found by a low moaning they were alive – they were in fever, four children, a woman and what had once been a man. It is impossible to go through the detail. Suffice it to say, that in a few minutes I was surrounded by at least 200 such phantoms, such frightful spectres as no words can describe, [suffering] either from famine or from fever. Their demoniac yells are still ringing in my ears, and their horrible images are fixed upon my brain.

People who had been reasonably healthy deteriorated to skin and bones in the space of four weeks, probably because of the ravages of dysentery. There were reports of 'walking skeletons'. Entire families, evicted from their homes, died by the roadside. Many of those who died lay unburied, or were buried, unshrouded and uncoffined, in shallow graves, and were gnawed at by rats and dogs. The frozen ground was usually too hard to dig, and the survivors were too weak to dig it. In some places huge

FUNERAL AT SKIBBEREEN From a sketch by Mr. H. Smith, Cork.

trenches were dug as mass graves, and the dead were thrown in and covered with quicklime, to aid in the decomposition of the bodies and prevent infection.

Trevelyan's public works schemes required funding by locally raised taxes, with food sold to those employed on the schemes by local traders. However, the revenue raised was insufficient, and people were used to bartering goods and labour rather than buying and selling. They found it difficult to deal with the commercial exchange required to convert their cash to food. Without enthusiastic government backing of the public works schemes they were instituted haphazardly. In some areas that they were operational at all was due to the tireless efforts of local clergy and landlords, who knew that without paid employment people would starve.

From the end of December until June 1847 when the public works scheme began to be wound down and was replaced with soup kitchens, up to 700,000 men, women and children were working on the roads, but the pittance they earned couldn't keep pace with food prices that were rising daily. Workers were supposed to be paid at the end of each day, but the pay lists were frequently delayed and days went by without any wages being paid out. Without payment, no food could be bought, so people often worked for several days without eating, frequently having

WORKHOUSE food fight

walked up to six miles to work and back again. Many collapsed and died during their heavy work assignments. Children were often the first casualties – any food that could be afforded was reserved for the men so that they could keep working.

Food shortages were widespread across northern Europe during 1846, and most of the grain imported from America and southern Europe was diverted to northern Europe where higher prices could be achieved. Trevelyan insisted that the problem with food distribution was not lack of money but lack of available food.

> The stock of food for the whole United Kingdom is much less than is required; and if we were to purchase for Irish use faster than we are now doing, we should commit a crying injustice to the rest of the country.

The Irish infrastructure was sadly lacking and any food that did find its way into the country was not easy to distribute to the hardest-hit areas in the west and southwest of the country, where people had been completely dependent on the potato for their food. When the Inspector General of the British Coastguard, Sir James Dombrain, distributed food to some starving people he encountered he was upbraided by Trevelyan, who told him that he should instead have encouraged the Irish to form a local committee to raise funds with which to buy food. 'There was none who could have contributed one shilling ... The people were actually dying,' was the retort.

Shipments of Indian corn began to arrive in the spring of 1846, but hardly anyone could afford to buy it and it was stored in harbour warehouses while people languished, starving, in the surrounding streets. Processing the corn also proved problematic – few mills in Ireland had the capacity to grind it and some of it was shipped to England for milling. The authorities made an attempt to revive the use of the hand-mill, or quern, but this was unsuccessful, except in Kilkee, County Clare, where a man was found who undertook to make and sell the ancient type of mill.

The workhouses quickly filled up with those who qualified for 'indoor relief' under the Poor Law – the property qualification had been reduced to such an extent by the infamous 'Gregory Clause' (see page 173) that for most people the only way to gain admission to the workhouse was to sell whatever small piece of land they owned, thus ensuring that more acreage was available for pasture. Even then, the workhouse was no guarantee of survival and seeking admission was the very last resort of an increasingly desperate population.

In April 1848 Charles Trevelyan was knighted by Queen Victoria for his contribution to famine relief.

The Situation Worsens

There is woe, there is clamour, in our desolated land.

From 'A Lament for the Potato',
Lady Jane 'Speranza' Wilde

By the beginning of 1847, the numbers employed on the various public works schemes had swelled to 700,000. The system lent itself to corruption and the success of the scheme varied widely from place to place. Since it was administered locally, those places with absentee landlords drew the short straw, as there was no competent person to take on the organisation of the various initiatives. Thus, the worst-off areas fared least well – hard-hit Skibbereen in West Cork was a case in point. Those approved to work on the schemes were sometimes those in least need – farmers with some means and even animals that they could rent out as beasts of burden were employed ahead of those in desperate circumstances.

It had soon become clear that the truly needy were not earning enough to buy the food that would stave off starvation until such time as the potato harvest returned to normal.

With reports that people had dropped dead while working on relief schemes, and accounts of the dreadful weather conditions in which they were expected to work, all graphically illustrated by the *Illustrated London News*, government policy on famine relief was denounced as inadequate and unfeeling by many intellectuals and liberal thinkers, within Ireland and in the rest of Britain. Oscar Wilde's mother Jane, a staunch supporter of the Young Ireland movement, was one of these. She was loud in her condemnation of government policies that had brought the people of Europe's most fertile land to their knees. Her poem, 'A Lament for the Potato', was published in *The Nation* early that year:

LADY JANE WILDE, also known as Speranza, mother of Oscar Wilde

There is woe, there is clamour, in our desolated land,
And wailing lamentation from a famine stricken band;
And weeping are the multitudes in sorrow and despair,
For the green fields of Munster lying desolate and bare.
Woe for Lorc's ancient kingdom, sunk in slavery and grief;
Plundered, ruined, are our gentry, our people, and their Chief;
For the harvest lieth scattered, more worth to us than gold,
All the kindly food that nourished both the young and the old.

Well I mind me of the cosherings, where princes might dine,
And we drank until nightfall the best seven sorts of wine;
Yet was ever the Potato our old, familiar dish,
And the best of all sauces with the beeves and the fish.
But the harp now is silent, no one careth for the sound;
No flowers, no sweet honey, and no beauty can be found;
Not a bird its music trilling through the leaves of the wood,
Nought but weeping and hands wringing in despair for our food.

The government reacted to the mounting criticism by changing tack, finally acknowledging that it should be working to keep the people alive by feeding them rather than reducing their life expectancy with hard labour for totally inadequate wages.

In January 1847 Prime Minister Russell addressed the House of Commons on the necessity of introducing a better system of providing relief.

> … the destitution and the want of food had so greatly increased, that it was desirable to attempt some other temporary scheme, by which, if possible, some of the evils which they have now to meet might be mitigated, and with so vast an expenditure of money that more effectual relief should be afforded. … it will be desirable to form in districts … relief committees, which relief committees shall be empowered to receive subscriptions, levy rates and receive donations from the government;

PRIME MINISTER RUSSELL, Engraved by Holl, from a photograph by Mayall, 1875.

that by means of these they should purchase food and establish soup kitchens in the different districts; that they should, so far as they are able, distribute rations with the purchased food to the famishing inhabitants, and that, furnishing that food, they should not require as indispensable the test of work, but that labouring men should be allowed to work on their own plots of ground … and thus tend to produce food for the next harvest. …

SATIRE IN PUNCH, entitled the 'political pas de quatre', with Daniel O'Connell, Robert Peel, John Russell and an unnamed fourth person

we must take care that the substitution of this system for public works shall be made as easy in the transition as possible.

In February 1847 this forward-thinking recommendation became law when the government passed the Poor Relief (Ireland) Act. It provided a mechanism for replacing the scheme of public works with a system of 'outdoor relief', which would set up soup kitchens, run by local relief committees, to feed the starving poor. The Poor Law that was operational at this time was extended under the act to provide the funds for the scheme. However, the functioning of the Poor Law in any given area depended on subscriptions being raised from the landowners in that locality, and it was a way of forcing absentee landlords to put their hands in their pockets to provide for their tenantry. When a petition was sent from Cork to the prime minister in the autumn by people fearful of another hard winter with no food, he was categorical about where the duty to fund relief lay.

The owners of property in Ireland should feel the obligation of feeding the poor … It is not just to expect the working classes of Great Britain should permanently support the burden of Irish pauperism.

As the famine became entrenched, more and more tenants defaulted on their rents – regardless of whether landlords took the cruel decision to evict the defaulters, they themselves had less and less income, and many of them had mortgages on their properties. There was, therefore, little money to be raised under the Poor Law, so the soup kitchens were mainly funded by government grants and private philanthropic subscriptions instead. The economy

MOVEEN, COUNTY CLARE, destroyed during evictions

of the country was generally in bad shape – business and commerce were grinding to a halt.

The food provided by the soup kitchens was of poor quality and the recipes used were not suitable for starving digestive systems – people suffered severe bowel problems – and, most devastating of all, there wasn't enough food to meet the demand. People had to be inspected as to their eligibility for outdoor relief and sometimes had to travel more than 20 miles for the inspection, an enormous distance for people who were starving. An incident was reported in Mayo where five people were found dead on the road on the morning after such an inspection.

> The bodies of these ill-fated creatures lay exposed on the road side for three or four days and nights, for the dogs and ravens to feed upon, until some charitable person had them buried in a turf hole at the road side.

In Dublin, where the population had increased dramatically when people swarmed into the city looking for work, the soup kitchens were inundated. In 1847 a celebrated philanthropic and self-promoting French chef (probably the first celebrity chef in history), Alexis Soyer, having corresponded with the *Times* of London on the subject of the necessity of feeding the starving people of Ireland, took some time out from his position at the Reform Club in London to set up a soup kitchen in a temporary wooden structure in front of the Royal Barracks at Arbour Hill. His aim was to provide a soup for the poor for as little money as possible. The great and the good of Dublin attended the opening of the venture, but those not issued with invitations were charged an admission fee of five shillings (which was used to defray the costs of the soup).

The soup kitchen was a temporary wooden structure, furnished with a huge 1,100-litre steam-operated cauldron and an enormous coal-fired bread oven. The recipients of the soup queued outside in a sort of zigzag formation to reduce the risk of contamination with the famine-related diseases that were becoming rife. Every six minutes people were admitted in relays – when a bell

ALEXIS SOYER

rang, 100 people were allowed into the building.
They were each given a bowl of soup, which they
ate with spoons that were chained to the tables.
When they had finished the soup, everyone was
given a ration of a single piece of bread and exited
through a second door. The bell rang again and the
next group was admitted. After the inauguration
day, the *Freeman's Journal* was scathing about the
proceedings.

M.SOYER'S model
soup kitchen,
Dublin

> … of all the impudent and insulting
> humbugs that ever were perpetrated against
> a suffering people, we hold the exhibition of
> yesterday, at the Royal Barracks, to have been
> the most outrageous.

In the context of Victorian Britain, where the
well-heeled and curious were routinely taken on
tours of prisons and slums for their amusement,
the 'exhibition' would not have been an unusual
initiative, although the spectacle of genteel ladies

in crinolines milling around sites of abject misery must have been bizarre.

In the aftermath of the opening day, Soyer's kitchen had a fairly short existence, but it fed in the region of 8,750 people each day while it was up and running, considerably more than the estimated 5,000. The soup recipe was basic and contained few ingredients – the protein content was minimal. However, it was hot and provided some sustenance, and a remarkable 100 gallons could be prepared for the modest sum of £1. His soup recipe was published in the *Times*.

> I first put one ounce of dripping into a sauce-pan (capable of holding two gallons of water), with a quarter of a pound of leg beef without bones, cut into square pieces about half an inch, and two middle-sized onions, peeled and sliced. I then set the saucepan over a coal fire, and stirred the contents round for a few minutes with a wooden (or iron) spoon until fried lightly brown. I had then ready washed the peeling of two turnips, fifteen green leaves or tops of celery, and the green part of two leeks (the whole of which, I must observe, are always thrown away). Having cut the above vegetables into small pieces, I threw them into the

saucepan with the other ingredients, stirring them occasionally over the fire for another ten minutes; then added half a pound of common flour (any farinaceous substance would do), and half a pound of pearl barley, mixing all well together. I then added two gallons of water, seasoned with three ounces of salt, and a quarter of an ounce of brown sugar, stirred occasionally until boiling, and allowed it to simmer very gently for three hours, at the end of which time I found the barley perfectly tender.

ALEXIS SOYER'S
magic stove

According to Soyer, this soup 'has been tasted by numerous noblemen, members of Parliament, and several ladies, who have lately visited my kitchen department, and who have considered it very good and nourishing'. The recipe appeared in *Soyer's Charitable Cookery*, which he published while in Ireland, donating the proceeds to charity.

CELEBRITY CHEF ALEXIS SOYER published several popular cookbooks

The poor-quality soup that had been served in the earlier government-sponsored soup kitchens was soon replaced with a type of gruel, or porridge, prepared with rice and Indian cornmeal. At the height of their operation, the soup kitchens were feeding some three million people on a regular basis. Wage earners were expected to contribute towards the cost of the food, but 'destitute helpless persons' and 'destitute able-bodied persons', who owned little or no land, qualified for free rations.

Towards the end of 1846, the Irish Quakers, realising that there would probably be a hiatus between the winding down of the public works initiatives and the setting up of food relief schemes in the form of soup kitchens, took it upon themselves to instigate famine relief measures that were completely independent of any government assistance. Rather than wringing their hands at the scale of the problem, they set about doing what they could. Their maxim was 'if there be one thousand of our fellow-men who would perish if nothing be done, our rescue of one hundred from destruction is surely not the less a duty and a privilege, because there are another nine hundred whom we cannot save'. They were less inclined to lay the blame at the door of Divine Providence than were other Christians. A Quaker who was active in the famine relief initiative, William Bennett, asked, pointedly,

STARVING PEASANTS living outside with no shelter

> Is this to be regarded in the light of a Divine dispensation and punishment? Before we can safely arrive at such a conclusion, we must be satisfied that human agency and legislation, individual oppressions, and social relationships have had no hand in it.

In the autumn of 1846 the Quakers set up independent soup kitchens, funded by subscriptions from their own religious community. The small population of Quakers (around 3,000 in the middle of the 19th century) was concentrated in the south-east of the country, so there were logistical difficulties in getting aid to those western areas of the country that were worst affected by famine. Despite these difficulties, theirs was a well-organised relief effort, with a central committee in Dublin that liaised with satellite groups around the country and had links to the Quaker community in England. Their aid was not limited to soup kitchens, but to donations of clothing, food and money with which to buy food, and they also funded non-Quakers who were operating separate relief initiatives. Clothing was often made by the people who donated it, and some came from factories that were applied to for donations by the Quaker women's committees.

The Quaker community was not large, and people had subscribed whatever they could when approached in 1846. Although it became clear during the harsh winter of 1846–47 that help would be needed on an ongoing basis, the coffers were emptying, which put the soup kitchens in jeopardy. However, a lot of lateral thinking had been applied to the problem and much of the Quaker approach was forward-looking and modern: seed was distributed to communities where even the seed potatoes had been eaten; fishing nets were donated to fishermen who had sold the means of their livelihood in order to buy some food. The Quakers also supported local employment schemes, frequently in the area of textile production, which was a traditional Quaker area of endeavour.

Evangelical Protestants, who had been particularly active in the west of Ireland for several decades, made offers of food, clothing or money to people in return for their conversion from Catholicism. For those who accepted, the taint of 'souperism' was ostracising, but the practice was not as widespread as famine mythology suggests.

Canon O'Rourke reported that 1846 'closed in gloom. It left the Irish people sinking in thousands into their graves, under the influence of a famine as general as it was intense … But the worst had not yet come.' Until then, Skibbereen in Cork had been the area worst hit by the famine, but, according to O'Rourke, 'Ireland had now many Skibbereens … the greater part of it might be regarded as one vast Skibbereen.' Those whom starvation hadn't killed were picked off by fever. An account from Ennis in County Clare reported that 'the number of those who, from age or exhaustion and infirmity, are unable to labour, is becoming most alarming; to those the public works are of no use. Deaths are occurring from Famine, and there can be no doubt

AN EJECTED FAMILY,
Erskine Nicol,
1825–1904

that the Famine advances upon us with giant strides.' Efforts to feed the starving poor had largely failed. A harrowing account sent that winter from the area near Belfast paints a grim picture.

> I entered a house to which my attention had been directed; in the kitchen there was not a single article of furniture – not even a live cinder on the cold deserted-looking hearth. In the inner room I found a woman, lately confined, lying upon a heap of chopped-up rotten straw, with scarcely a rag to cover her; beside her nestled two children, pictures of want, and in her bosom lay her undressed babe, that, four days before, had first seen the light. She had no food in the house, nor had she, nor her children, had anything since her confinement, save a little soup procured from the public kitchen. Such was her statement; and the evidence of her wretched dwelling bore but too ample testimony to her melancholy tale.

In 1847, the potato harvest was free from blight, but was very insubstantial. The people had failed to store enough seed potatoes and had no money with which to buy them. They were frequently so weakened by hunger that they didn't have the strength to plant them

MICK MCQUAID'S Cabin, Connemara, County Galway, photograph from the late 19th century

even if they had any. Despite the Quaker distribution of vegetable seeds there were not enough planted to provide a replacement crop. The famine continued into 1848, and people were already so debilitated that they died in greater numbers than before, despite the various relief schemes in operation. The eyewitness accounts from 1847 are harrowing. In Clifden, almost the entire population was attempting to live on seaweed. In a letter to the central committee of the Society of Friends, James Tuke wrote:

BURYING THE CHILD

Oil painting by Lillian Lucy Davidson (1879–1954)

During that period, the roads in many places became as charnel-houses, and several car and coach drivers have assured me that they rarely drove anywhere without seeing dead bodies strewn along the road side, and that, in the dark, they had even gone over them. A gentleman told me that in the neighbourhood of Clifden one Inspector of roads caused no less than 140 bodies to be buried, which he had found scattered along the highway. In some cases it is well known that where all other members of a family have perished, the last survivor has earthed up the door of his miserable cabin to prevent the ingress of pigs and dogs, and then laid himself down to die in this fearful family vault.

Although some landlords helped their tenants, many (usually absentees) did not, and evictions for non-payment of rent were rife. For some it was an opportunity to clear their lands of their tenantry and free them up for pasture. More than 20 years after

KEILLINES, Galway, near General Thompson's property

the famine Canon O'Rourke asked a 'gentleman who knew the Midland Counties and portions of the west well', what were 'the feelings of the landlords with regard to the tenants dying of starvation?' 'DELIGHTED TO BE RID OF THEM', was the reply.

People with no other means of sustaining themselves applied for admission to the workhouses in the hope that they could cling to life until food became available again. In 1848, the blight reappeared and the potato harvest was lost again. The crop failed again in 1849 – It was 1850, a full five years after the first blighted potato crop, before the blight finally disappeared.

CORK SOCIETY OF FRIENDS'
Soup House

The Role of the Workhouse During the Great Famine

...the people must not be suffered to starve in the midst of plenty ...

Undated letter from the parish priest of Kenmare, County Kerry, to Trevelyan

During the years of the famine, much of the relief made available to those affected was through the operation of the Poor Law. A government commission of inquiry set up in 1833 estimated that in excess of two million people in Ireland would need some assistance for several weeks each year. A form of poor law had been in existence in England since the beginning of the 17th century, but it had never been instituted in Ireland. The Poor Law was a charge, or rate, on property owners – the assistance encompassed by the law was 'outdoor', making provision for people who were living as part of the general population.

In 1834, in an attempt to reduce the amount of money paid out under the Poor Law, relief was often limited to accommodation in workhouses, the so-called 'indoor relief'. In 1838 a Poor Law was enacted for Ireland, as part of an initiative to move people off their smallholdings, in the interests of encouraging agriculture on an industrial scale. A portion of the legislation related to assistance with emigration. Ireland, however, was not an industrial powerhouse like her nearest neighbour – the economy was largely agrarian, and the poor lived mainly on potatoes. Poor Law relief was charged locally on landowners – the 'rate' was essentially a tax – but, as the famine took hold, people defaulted on their rents, and the income of the landlords fell dramatically. Unlike the captains of industry and major landowners in England, Irish landowners were badly placed to contribute to the relief of their former tenants.

The Irish Poor Law provided for the establishment of 130 'unions' around the country,

MOTHER AND CHILD wait outside a workhouse

based on the more than 2,000 townlands (a townland is a peculiarly Irish division, describing an area of 120 acres) around the country. A workhouse was to be set up in each union in a central location that would be equally accessible to all residents in a particular area. The purchase of sites and the building of the workhouses would be covered by monies from the exchequer, but the operational funding was to come from the poor rate.

The building of the workhouse network in Ireland began at the beginning of 1839. An English architect, George Wilkinson, who had already designed workhouses in England, was commissioned to inspect the proposed sites and design all 130 Irish workhouses. His annual salary was £500. Spending on construction would be tightly controlled.

> The style of building is intended to be of the cheapest description compatible with durability; and effect is aimed at by harmony of proportion and simplicity of arrangement, all mere decoration being studiously excluded.

Wilkinson quickly drew up plans, and these were reproduced for each of the workhouses around the country. There was to be strict gender segregation within the building complexes, with separate accommodation for men and women and a 'Master' and 'Matron' *in situ*. This was further divided into accommodation for the elderly, the infirm and 'idiots'. Children's dormitories were usually upstairs and classrooms were also provided for. Receiving rooms at the front of the buildings were used to accommodate new arrivals until they were processed. There was a kitchen, a laundry, an infirmary and a store for the inmates' own clothing (one commentator bemoaned the fact that at the height of the famine, there was no workhouse clothing to distribute to new arrivals, who had to wear their own clothes). The dining-room doubled as the workhouse chapel.

THE WORKHOUSE,
Clifden, Connemara

By 1843, 112 workhouses had been finished, with the remainder nearing completion. However, in many areas the poor rate hadn't been collected so the workhouses couldn't open their doors.

In England the Poor Law covered outdoor relief, but in Ireland its application was restricted to indoor relief, so that outside the workhouse no assistance would be available. The Irish Poor Law mirrored the English in that it was established to provide temporary relief for those who were completely destitute – it had no role to play in the alleviation of general poverty, except insofar as the workhouse infirmaries were allowed to treat those who were merely poor. Although famine had been a feature of life in Ireland during previous centuries, there was no provision in the law to take account of extraordinary circumstances, such as when destitution affected large numbers of the population. The provision for 130 workhouses, capable of accommodating about 100,000 people in total, was the limit of the assistance envisaged.

A FORMER workhouse in Dunfanaghy, Donegal, one of many still standing.

As with much early welfare provision, any help that was provided was deliberately kept at a level that made it less attractive than a wage – this was known as the principle of 'less eligibility'. Workhouses applied a regime that was little better than that of the prisons of the time. Would-be inmates were interviewed as to their suitability and eligibility, then they were bathed and given a workhouse uniform. Families were split up as soon as they arrived – men, women and children over two years of age were all housed separately, with little opportunity for any family time. The able-bodied had to work – men at rock-breaking, women at knitting or sewing. Smoking, which might have provided comfort to some, was prohibited.

The inmates' days were monotonous and unvarying. Their regime was dictated by the sound of the bell. At 6.00 every morning the bell rang to wake them. It rang again at 6.30 for roll call, followed by breakfast. After breakfast, the adults worked from 7.00 until 6.00 in the evening, and the

STARVING PEASANTS beseiging a workhouse gate

supper bell rang at 6.30. The bell rang for the final time at 8.30, signalling lights out.

There was provision for the education of children – the curriculum was limited to reading, writing and arithmetic – the three 'Rs' – and religious education. The mornings were spent in the schoolroom, and the afternoons were devoted to exercise. In practice the teachers were poorly trained and incapable of managing large classrooms; malnourished children found it difficult to engage in meaningful outdoor exercise. Substantial numbers of young children died in the workhouses during the famine, many of them alone, without the comfort of their families. By 1850 there were 120,000 children in the workhouses (these had been extended during the famine to cope with increasing demand), a large number of whom had been orphaned by the famine. With no one interested in their welfare they were malnourished, dirty and dressed in rags.

The sleeping accommodation was crowded and poorly ventilated, while the 'beds' were planks with thin straw mattresses and ragged blankets. There were no overnight toilet facilities, just big tubs in the middle of the dormitories that frequently overflowed with the urine of the inmates.

The diet, in keeping with the principle of 'less eligibility', proved contentious from the start. Given that the inmates had been used to living on a subsistence diet, it was difficult to provide something that was worse than their normal fare. There were two meals a day – breakfast consisted of oatmeal porridge and milk, and supper was potatoes and buttermilk. Some of the Dublin unions, dealing with a populace that was unused to the basic rural diet, exerted pressure on the Poor Law Commissioners to achieve the addition of some meat to the diet on two days each week. As the blight spread, oats, rice and bread were substituted for the more nutritious potato and soon inmates were being given whatever food was available in their union.

The poor rate increased in relation to the numbers of people sent to the workhouse. By the

WOMAN
begging in Clonakilty, County Cork, *London Illustrated News*

late 1840s the poor rate that was collected in the areas hardest hit by the blight produced food rations so poor and so paltry that it was said that inmates would commit crimes in order to be given prison sentences, which carried the advantage of the more sustaining prison rations.

WORKHOUSE
children were fed a limited diet

During the first years of their operation the workhouses were never full, and most of the inmates were elderly and infirm, or infants, with few able-bodied adults to swell their ranks. Even after the blight had made its first appearance in 1845, the workhouse population was as low as 38,000.

There were many cases of food hardship caused by crop failure in 1839 and again in 1842 – it was not widespread, but in the localities affected the difficulties were severe. Despite this, the Poor Law Commissioners, charged with the administration of the legislation, were adamant that there could be no temporary extension of relief.

By April 1846, people were feeling the effects of the prolonged food shortage and they began to apply for workhouse admission. By June of that year there were over 50,000 inmates, which meant that the entire workhouse network was filled to half capacity, although many of the workhouses in the worst affected areas were already full. The government had decided to continue the system

ONE OF SWINEFORD workhouse's inmates was Michael Davitt, founder of the Land League and an MP, who entered the workhouse at the age of four.

of temporary relief measures, with public works initiatives playing the most important role. The Poor Law Commissioners were instructed to estimate the requirement for workhouse accommodation in 1847 on the basis that they would not be filled to capacity. There was a great deal of official confidence in the ability of the public works schemes to provide relief and it was thought that most of those applying for admission to the workhouses would be those who were too old or too infirm to work.

The confidence of the commissioners was misplaced. By the end of the second year of the potato blight, more than half of Ireland's workhouses were full. It was the coldest winter in living memory, the public works schemes paid poorly and irregularly and food prices were continuing to rise, throwing more people on the mercy of the Poor Law and its workhouses. In November 1846 a Quaker relief worker issued a report on the conditions at Swineford (now Swinford) workhouse in County Mayo:

On the dreadful 10th November 120 were admitted beyond the regulated number. Hundreds were refused admission for want of room, some unhappy persons being pushed on the high roads and in the fields. Influenced by terror and dismay – leaving entire districts almost deserted – the better class of farmers, in numbers, sold their property, at any sacrifice, and took flight to America. And the humbler classes left the country in masses, hoping to find a happier doom in any other region. In this Union 367 persons died in the workhouse:

THE WORKHOUSE infirmaries had a high incidence of disease and death.

the Master of the workhouse also died. In the adjoining Union, Ballina, 200 were admitted to the workhouse beyond the number it was built for (1,200). Hundreds were refused admission for want of room and 1,138 died in the workhouse; the medical officer of the workhouse was also carried off. In another adjoining Union, Ballinasloe, all the officers

MISS KENNEDY
distributes clothing to the poor at Kilrush 1849.

of the workhouse were swept away, and 254 inmates of the workhouse perished.

On Christmas Eve 1846 the District Commissioner in Sligo gave a harrowing account of scenes he had encountered:

> I witnessed the women and little children, crowds of whom were to be seen scattered over the turnip fields, like a flock of famished crows, devouring the raw turnips, mothers half naked, shivering in the snow and sleet, uttering exclamations of despair whilst their children were screaming with hunger … The workhouse is full, and police are stationed at the doors to keep the numberous applicants out …

By the spring of 1847, workhouse occupancy was running at 75 per cent across the country.

Those unions in the worst affected areas were inundated with applications for admission – already full to capacity, they had to turn scores of people away. There was no provision for the transfer of applicants from one union to another – if the local workhouse was full, people were not allowed to travel to another to seek admission. This

rule was also applied to the fever hospitals, most of which were part of the workhouse structure.

When a workhouse was full, it became the practice of the guardians to issue a notice suspending any new admissions. The notice in Roscommon read:

> … the State of the Poor House … makes it absolutely necessary for the Guardians to proclaim the utter impossibility to admit any more persons until further notice.
>
> The Guardians have on two occasions given a small portion of Bread to disappointed applicants; but after this Notice, it can never be done again, such expenditure being illegal …

The parish priest of Kenmare in County Kerry was moved to write to Trevelyan of the plight of his parishioners and the inefficacy of the system established by the government for their relief:

A STARVING FAMILY in front of their sod house.

Would to God that you could stand for one five minutes in our street, and see with what a troop of miserable, squalid, starving creatures you would be instantaneously surrounded, with tears in their eyes and with misery in their faces, imploring and beseeching you to get them a place in the workhouse … Whatever be the cost or expense, or on whatever party it may fall, every Christian must admit, that the people must not be suffered to starve in the midst of plenty, and that the first duty of a Government is to provide for the poor under the circumstances such as they are placed.

DESPERATE poverty-stricken people seek shelter in a workhouse in the west of Ireland.

The workhouse guardians, faced daily with the prospect of turning people away who had no other recourse, admitted so many that the workhouses were soon overcrowded. They also provided outdoor relief in the form of food donations, although this was expressly prohibited by the law. It was clear that more government aid was needed, but little was forthcoming until late 1846 when the workhouse guardians were allowed to find more accommodation to meet the demand. While the government agreed to pay for the acquisition of the properties, the support of the inmates would, as always, have to come from the poor rate. Conditions in the overcrowded workhouses were dreadful and famine-associated fevers quickly took hold among the inmates and staff.

When the government soup kitchens were set up they took some of the pressure off the workhouses, but the relief system worked in such a way that people could be refused outdoor relief in the form of food if there was available accommodation in the local workhouse. A provision in the legislation to the effect that there was no right to relief under the Poor Law meant that for those turned away from the workhouse there was often no access to any other kind of relief under the legislation – the Poor Law Commissioners could wash their hands of the problems of such unfortunate people and throw them on the mercy of the government relief schemes.

By now, the public in Ireland and Britain, in the throes of an economic recession, were suffering from compassion fatigue. The destitute were moving from the Irish countryside to the larger urban centres in the hope of finding work and they were also travelling to England, thereby becoming a visible and unwanted problem. The newspapers were beginning to call for less rather than more government intervention – the *Times* of London declared that 'something like harshness is the greatest humanity'. A British economist, Nassau Senior, reflected on the altered mood of the time.

NASSAU SENIOR, an English lawyer and economist. For several decades he was a government adviser on economic and social policy.

> The English resolved that the Irish should not starve. We

resolved that, for one year at least, we would feed them. But we came to a third resolution, inconsistent with the first, that we would not feed them for more than a year. How then were they to be fed in 1848? Of course they must be supported by poor rates.

In the summer of 1847 Trevelyan engineered an extension to the Poor Law legislation 'for the season of 1847–48 and for all after-time'. A separate Irish Poor Law Commission was set up to look after the specific needs of the country in the extreme circumstances of the famine. The Poor Law unions were expanded from 130 to 163. For the first time in Ireland, outdoor relief would be supplied under the Poor Law, although the criteria for eligibility were strict. This was a major shift in government policy and the extension alarmed landowners, who were now required to shoulder the entire burden of relief – since 1843, any landholding valued at less than £4 was exempt from the poor rate, which meant that the

HENRY LABOUCHÈRE MP, 1st Baron Taunton, English politician. Chief Secretary for Ireland in 1846.

rate was due almost exclusively from the landlords themselves. One of the more controversial clauses in the amended legislation was the so-called 'Gregory Clause', introduced by William Gregory, MP for Dublin (and husband of Lady Augusta Gregory). It restricted relief to those who occupied less than a quarter of an acre, or a rood (just over 1,000 square metres) of land. Many people simply left their land in order to qualify for relief, and many who were slow to take that drastic step were evicted for non-payment of their rent. As non rate-payers, they were a double drain on the landlords' resources.

The Gregory Clause facilitated the policy of land clearance. Henry Labouchère MP wrote to the prime minister that

> [I]t is useless to disguise the truth that any great improvement in the social system of Ireland must be founded upon an extensive change in the present state of agrarian occupation, and that this change necessarily

WILLIAM GREGORY, MP Anglo-Irish writer and politician and husband of the better remembered Lady Augusta Gregory.

implies a long, continued and systematic ejectment of small holders and of squatting cottiers.

By late 1848 close to a million people were getting workhouse relief – the expansion of the existing buildings and the construction of 33 additional workhouses had to cater for the vast increase in the number of people housed in the workhouses. That winter, the workhouse death rate was 2,500 people per week, with cholera the main culprit. Infectious diseases took hold very quickly in the crowded conditions of the workhouses and caused more deaths than hunger – malnourishment reduced the resistance of the inmates to disease.

During one week in a Cork workhouse, which was severely overcrowded, there was one death every hour. The high mortality rate meant that many of those who died in the workhouses were buried in communal graves – mothers were often buried with one of their children. The workhouse guardians generally tried to provide shrouds and coffins for all of the deceased (a proper burial was of great importance), but in some of the areas most overwhelmed, the 'sliding coffin' was used – this was placed in the grave with the deceased inside, but a hinged mechanism enabled the coffin to be removed for repeated use, leaving the corpse in the grave.

People were also dying in the streets, and there were no coffins in which to bury them. A priest wrote to the *Cork Examiner* about the plight of just one man, dying in his home. 'His sister and brother lay quite dead close to him in the same room. The sister was dead for five days, and the brother for three days. He also died, being the last of a large family. The three were interred by means of a sliding coffin.'

An alternative to the overcrowded workhouses or death at the side of the road was emigration – it would at once get rid of the financial burden of feeding the starving and clear the land of subsistence farmers to make way for the vast swathes of pasture envisaged by the government as part of the shift in agricultural policy.

DESTITUTE children scrabbling for scraps of food

The Diseases of the Famine

The matron, too, is dead ...
Report from Ballinrobe Workhouse,
County Mayo, March 1847

Famine and disease made frequent appearances in Ireland during the 18th and 19th centuries – where the first manifested itself, the second soon followed. Eminent medical people, including Dublin ophthalmologist Sir William Wilde (husband of Speranza and father of Oscar), recognised the prevalence of fever in Ireland as a 'scourge'. During the worst years of the Great Famine, 1845–49, a million people died of hunger and disease.

The main infections were tuberculosis, endemic typhus fever, dysentery and smallpox, at that time still a virulent killer. Scurvy was also common – potatoes are rich in vitamin C, the main preventer of scurvy, and when they were not available, scurvy struck even those who were receiving daily food rations of oatmeal porridge or bread, and the 'well-cooked' vegetables (cooking destroys vitamin C) recommended by the Poor Law Commissioners who had oversight of the workhouse diet. Vitamin C is not stored by the body, so a daily intake is essential. Lack of vitamin A (available in whole milk, but not in the skimmed milk that was provided in the workhouses) caused an eye disease called xerophthalmia, which affected children particularly, and can cause blindness in one eye. A non-fatal but painful skin condition, pellagra, was also prevalent, caused by the lack of some of the B vitamins and common in people whose main diet is Indian cornmeal.

Fever affected rich and poor alike, but those who enjoyed a good diet and hygienic living conditions were better equipped to recover from it. When it struck the poor they were doubly disabled, even if they survived, by the course of the disease, and by their inability to work while in a weakened state. Families already living on a knife edge were tipped into abject poverty.

DUBLIN OPHTHALMOLOGIST
Dr William Wilde.

THE IRISH FAMINE,
1850, by George
Frederick Watts
(1817-1904)

Nobody knew what caused fever to spread. Various theories were advanced – some people even thought it was due to the Indian corn that was being imported – but it was believed that famine was a primary cause. It is more likely that it was the filthy conditions in which people lived, their lack of access to warm clothing and fuel in the winter, and immune systems debilitated by extreme hunger, that allowed infectious diseases to take such a hold.

Typhus is now known to be carried by the louse – it can enter the body through skin lesions or by being inhaled. It can also gain access through the conjunctival membrane of the eye. It causes a high fever, rash, aching limbs and mental confusion. Those who died from it usually lasted two weeks until their hearts failed.

Another type of fever, relapsing fever, was the most common fever during the famine years. It is characterised by fever, aches and pains, nausea, jaundice and nosebleeds. The fever spikes after about a week and then the body temperature drops

and the patient becomes ravenously hungry. Symptoms return after about a week. The disease usually ran its course after several relapses, but those weakened by extreme hunger had no resources with which to fight prolonged bouts of fever. The fever made them very susceptible to dysentery, also known as the 'bloody flux', and diarrhoea.

Dysentery is a bacillus, spread by flies or infected water, but a weakened digestive system predisposes people to infection. The symptoms are stinking diarrhoea – sometimes with bloody stools – nausea, aching limbs, a reduced heart rate and shivering. It took hold among the destitute in the harsh winter of 1846–47. Those affected felt very cold, and if the diarrhoea continued unchecked, they wasted away until they resembled living skeletons and then died.

Smallpox, now eradicated worldwide, made an appearance in several epidemics during the famine. Fever, headache, aches and pains and an itchy purulent rash are characteristic; internal haemhorraging was the cause of death for most victims. Those who survived were often scarred, blind or infertile.

Pulmonary tuberculosis (TB) is another disease that afflicts the poor and hungry. Highly contagious, it rapidly travelled from one family member to another in the cramped, airless cabins in which

A SCENE FROM Mullins' hut, Schull 1847, from the *Illustrated London News*. A gentleman watches over a dying family.

the poor lived at the time of the famine. The symptoms are coughing, eventually producing blood, with chest pain, fever, night sweats and chills. Malnutrition increases susceptibility to TB.

Fear of infection was great – during the first half of the 19th century a number of fever hospitals were built around the country,

although not in all areas. Many residents objected strenuously to the construction of such hospitals close to centres of population. Despite this, between early 1847 and the summer of that year there was a demand for temporary fever hospitals where the infected could be isolated – almost 400 requests for

A HUT in the old Chapel Yard, refuge for the sick and dying

such structures were granted. Local fever hospitals were funded through local taxes, and the fever hospital/infirmary accommodation in the workhouses built when the Poor Law was extended to Ireland in 1838 were also funded by the poor rate. In areas where there was no provision for a fever hospital, those infected were quarantined at home or in 'fever huts', stone or mud huts hastily erected at the side of the road or in the corner of a field. The sick were frequently left to their own devices – in the absence of medical attention and nursing care, if disease didn't kill them, they were often carried off by hunger and thirst.

In June 1847 a constable in Aughrim in County Wicklow, torn between compassion and the practical requirements of his employment, wrote a harrowing account of a fever-stricken woman and child he came upon on the roadside on his beat.

> … a travelling pauper named Honor Kerwin and her child dropped on the highway near Aughrim, both being ill with fever and lay on the side of the road till the following day when I reported the case to Jeremiah Tool the warden, who had them conveyed to Rathdrum Fever Hospital immediately. But being refused admittance there they were sent back to this place and left on the cross roads at Aughrim the most past of the night and

then put into a shed. On the following day … I informed Doctor Atkins of the case who gave a certificate stating the poor woman had a fever and was a fit object for the Fever Hospital.

The Revd Mr Malony and two [rate payers] recommended them to the Fever Hospital also. These recommendations together with the warden's note was forwarded the same day, with the poor woman, to Arklow Fever Hospital and [she] was refused admittance there stating they should 'have been sent to Rathdrum' and had them conveyed back to Aughrim and left on the cross roads for a night to the great danger of the people of this neighbourhood.

On Tuesday myself and two of this party with some others of the neighbours procured timber and erected a shed and put the two sick persons in to it and went through the neighbours and got a few pence to get them nourishment for them and also procured a nurse tender to take care of them. It is a very hard case that there is no place to remove poor persons of this description when they fall on the public roads and although I am well aware it is

no part of my duty to interfere in such cases. Still every
person calls me to keep the public passways clear of such
nuisances. There is 8 or 9 families at present ill with fever in
this neighbourhood, some of them in sheds and no place to
receive them.

If families had a slightly more substantial dwelling house, those
affected by fever were often walled away in one room of the house,
and a hole was made in the outside wall for the doctor to crawl
through. Not surprisingly, medical personnel contracted fever at a
high rate.

As the famine progressed, conditions in the workhouses, workhouse
infirmaries and fever hospitals were so crowded and unhygienic that
infections spread through the patients and inmates like wildfire. Those
who gained admission to the workhouses were often issued with
the unwashed uniforms of those who had died, providing infectious
diseases with more opportunities for spreading.

A report from Ballinrobe in County Mayo in March 1847 described
the workhouse there as being

… in the most awfully deplorable state, pestilence having attacked paupers, officers, and all. In fact, this building is one horrible charnel house, the unfortunate paupers being nearly all the victims of a fearful fever, the dying and the dead, we might say, huddled together. The master has become a victim of this dread disease … the matron, too, is dead.

Now the Ballinrobe board have complied with the Commissioners' orders, in admitting a houseful of paupers and in striking a new rate, which cannot be collected; while the unfortunate inmates, if they escape the awful epidemic, will survive only to be the subjects of a lingering death by starvation.

… the paupers are dying in dozens.

In May 1847, when people were dying as fast as the survivors could bury them, the Dublin Board of Health issued guidelines for the prevention of the spread of fever – it laid down rules for admission to fever hospitals, including one that demanded that all applicants for outdoor relief should come to the distribution centres with 'at least face, hands and hair clean'. Given the conditions in which people were living it would have been almost impossible for them to comply with even this

simple requirement. The precautions were to no avail
– little could be done to improve the cramped and
unhygienic living conditions of the poor and disease
spread at an alarming pace.

The incidence of fever eventually reduced, but
this was due more to death and emigration than to
any improvement in conditions or medicine.

DISTRESS AT A home in Gorumna Island, County Galway, an image published in 1880

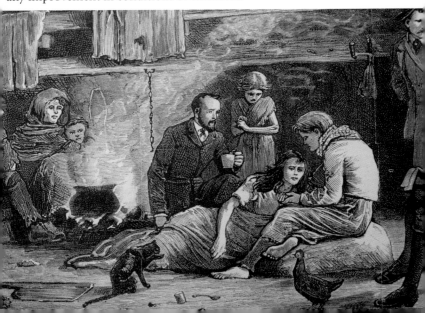

Eviction and Emigration

The Almighty indeed sent the potato blight, but the English created the Famine.

John Mitchel, Irish nationalist

There is no doubt that the potato blight was timely for some landlords and members of the British administration hell-bent on clearing estates of low-rent cottiers and labourers so that agriculture could be transformed from tillage to pasture. The evictions, or 'clearances', that became symbolic of the cruelty of the British administration and the propertied classes during the famine, had in fact been going on for decades in an attempt to convert Ireland's largely arable land cultivation to more profitable grazing. Only the tenant farmers, smallholders and cottiers stood in the way of progress, and many in Britain and Ireland believed the famine to be providential – literally sent by Providence to rid them of unprofitable tenants.

Canon O'Rourke gave an account of a Protestant judge who was appalled at the destitution he had encountered on his travels throughout the countryside in the winter of 1846–47. The judge wrote a bald assessment to the Dublin newspapers.

JOHN MITCHEL,
Irish nationalist
activist, author and
political journalist

> The potato cultivation being extinguished, at least for a time, the peasant cultivators can pay no rents, sheep and horned cattle can pay rents, and smart rents too; therefore the sheep and cattle shall have the lands, and the peasants shall be ousted from them … a universal system of ousting the peasantry is about to set in. Whether this results from the fault or from the necessities of the landlords it matters not.

Before the famine, evicting landlords ran the risk of being attacked and murdered by members of secret societies that were formed to resist the policy of eviction. Those weakened by hunger and disease had few resources at their disposal with which to resist – even so, 17 landlords were shot during the winter of 1846–47. The Lord Lieutenant, Lord Clarendon, asked Westminster for special powers with which to quash any rebellion – December 1847 saw the enactment of the Crime and Outrage Act. Clarendon laid the blame for the unrest squarely at the feet of the evicting landlords. 'It is quite true,' he wrote,

EVICTED FAMILY
seek shelter

… that landlords in England would not like to be shot like hares and partridges … but neither does any landlord in England turn out fifty persons at once and burn their houses over their heads …

It has been estimated, based on eviction notices actually served, that as many as half a million people were evicted from their homes in the nine years from 1846 to 1854. Clare and Mayo were the worst affected counties, with thousands of families summarily evicted from their homes. In 1847 the Catholic Bishop of Meath issued a pastoral letter on the subject of the evictions.

THE LORD LIEUTENANT, Lord Clarendon

Seven hundred human beings were driven from their homes in one day and set adrift on the world, to gratify the caprice of one who, before God and man, probably deserved less consideration than the last and least of them ... The horrid scenes I then witnessed, I must remember all my life long. The wailing of women – the screams, the terror, the consternation of children – the speechless agony of honest industrious men – wrung tears of grief from all who saw them. I saw officers and men of a large police force, who were obliged to attend on the occasion, cry like children at beholding the cruel sufferings of the very people whom they would be obliged to butcher had they offered the least

resistance. The landed proprietors in a circle all around – and for many miles in every direction – warned their tenantry, with threats of their direct vengeance, against the humanity of extending to any of them the hospitality of a single night's shelter ... and in little more than three years, nearly a fourth of them lay quietly in their graves.

The evictions continued long after the potato blight had disappeared and the Great Famine was officially over. Official records set the figure at only 250,000, but there were countless tenants who voluntarily surrendered their properties in order to qualify for the workhouse.

POLICE AND OFFICIALS preside over the destruction of a peasant cottage and the eviction of the family.

Conservative MP William Gregory's addition of the Quarter-Acre clause to the amended Poor Law regulations in 1847 ensured that all but the poorest cottiers were tempted to render themselves homeless so that their families could eat. The exclusion from Poor Law relief of all those holding a quarter of an acre of land or more led to a long debate within the Poor Law Commission in Dublin as to whether the dependants of such people could also be denied relief. In the middle of 1848 they finally agreed that the workhouse guardians could exercise discretion as to whether relief could be given in those cases.

Gregory has had his apologists, but his address to the House of Commons makes his disparagement of the Irish smallholder clear. Denying that his clause would destroy small famers in Ireland he said that if it could do that, he 'could not see of what use such small farmers could possibly be'. Canon O'Rourke was scathing in his assessment of the Gregory clause: 'A more complete engine for the slaughter and expatriation of a people was never designed.'

A FAMILY in Tipperary take shelter after an eviction. Engraving by Ebenezer Landells, 1848

It wasn't clear at first whether the dwelling was considered part of the property that had to be surrendered under the legislation, but many landlords and agents refused to rubber-stamp a tenant's surrender of his land until the house had also been surrendered, and workhouse guardians frequently refused to admit those who had surrendered their land but had not also given up their house. Where there was no voluntary surrender, famine-stricken families were often evicted for non-payment of rent. The debt was sometimes forgiven by landlords who just wanted to clear their land and turn it over to pasture, unencumbered by their cottiers and smallholders who were making no contribution to the Poor Law rate that was levied on the larger landholders.

Those homes that were surrendered or that had been the subject of an eviction order were destroyed, so that families could not creep back to them and, probably equally importantly, landlords would no longer be liable to pay a rate on them. At the height of the famine, when the workhouses were already overcrowded, evictions were effectively death sentences, and when they took place in the winter months, those evicted were liable to freeze to death. In April 1848 the *Waterford Chronicle* published a letter from the parish priest of Lismore, Father Patrick Fogarty, which summed up the situation of the evicted:

Numbers of these poor creatures who were thus cruelly exterminated are now living in huts erected by them on the roadside, victims of famine and fever. Hundreds of them have perished in these parishes during the last two years.

Despite the stakes being so high, there was no legal recourse against landlords who ordered evictions, and where a house was wrecked to prevent re-entry, the only claim that could be brought was in the civil courts, a course of action that was unlikely to be taken by dispossessed and starving people.

In October 1849 the *Illustrated London News* spoke up for the evicting landowners.

… however much we may deplore the misery from which they spring, and which they so dreadfully aggravate, we cannot compel the Irish proprietors to continue in their miserable holdings the wretched swarms of people who pay no rent, and who prevent the improvement of property so long as they remain upon it. … But it should be remembered that few of them have it in their power to be merciful or generous to their poorer tenantry … they are themselves engaged in a life and death struggle with their creditors.

Many of the clergy had been vocal in their condemnation of government policies throughout the years of the famine, and in relation to forced evictions and the deaths that were a direct result of them, the Roman Catholic Archbishop of Tuam wrote to Prime Minister Russell that

> … it seems, no matter what may be the amount of people's sufferings [evictions could continue to be carried out] … provided that nothing illegal or unconstitutional is done in vindicating the rights of property.

Irish landowners and their rights were well represented at Westminster. The foreign secretary, Lord Palmerston, expressed his belief that evictions were both necessary and acceptable in the quest to reform Irish agriculture, a view that was vociferously supported by the postmaster general, Lord Clanricarde. The prime minister was not so heartless – he wanted to stop, or at least to slow down the evictions: ' … the murders of poor cottier tenants are too horrible to bear, and if we put down assassins, we ought to put down the lynch law of the landlord'. Russell's cabinet was divided and he had little support for his views. His proposed legislation was watered down to the point of uselessness. The law that was passed provided for a mere slowing down in the rate of evictions; under the influence of the Irish peers in the House of Lords the notice period required was further reduced to a mere 48

'THE EJECTMENT'
of the Irish tenantry, *Illustrated London News*, 1848

THE POSTMASTER GENERAL, Lord Clanricarde

hours, and a prohibition on wrecking the home of an evicted tenant applied only if the tenant or his family were in the building at the time. Evictions on Christmas Day and Good Friday were also prohibited. Official records indicate that just under 141,000 families were turned out of their homes between 1846 and 1849, with the rate of evictions peaking in 1848.

Evictions were dreadful occasions, attended by the landlord or his agent and the sheriff. Up to 40 policemen and about 50 soldiers were assembled in the immediate vicinity to provide a deterrent against the likely threat of violence. An English Quaker, James Hack Tuke, in a secondhand account of the proceedings at an eviction, reported that those to be evicted pleaded to be allowed to remain, but the court order had been issued and there was no way back from that. A guest at a dinner party attended by the landlord who had evicted his tenants that day said that

SERVING SUMMONSES on the Clanricade Estate, Woodford, County Galway

the landowner had 'boasted that this was the first time he had seen the estate or visited the tenants'.

Sometimes those evicted were given small amounts of money, just enough to pay for a ticket on a boat to Liverpool, from where they hoped to find passage to the New World. However, many then remained in England, unable to afford the cost of travelling to the US or Australia. For some, passage to the New World was bought by their

evicting landlords, who were glad of the opportunity to export their unproductive tenants. For many of those evicted, the unknown risks of emigration were more attractive than starvation or subjection to the rigours of the workhouse.

Emigration had been a feature of Irish life for some time before the potato blight, with steady numbers of emigrants in the years before the Great Famine. Some of this was seasonal, with about 100,000 Irish migrating to Britain for the harvest each year. Many of these emigrants stayed on after the harvest, moving to the larger urban centres. Emigration featured more largely after the potato failure of 1822.

There were permanent emigrants to Britain, forced to leave Ireland where the system of land inheritance meant that increasingly small landholdings could afford to support only one or two siblings in a large family. Many of these emigrants worked as navvies on the construction of the network of canals in Britain between 1745 and 1840. When the great British railway building project began in 1830, it employed 200,000 Irish navvies.

In the second half of the 19th century more than a quarter of a million people left Ireland for various destinations. Most emigrants were male, and for many the destination of choice was England, but there was also encouragement to 'colonise' the territories of the New

World, often with the sweetener of financial aid. Between 1831 and 1841 the total emigration figure was 403,459, an annual average of just over 40,000. During that decade Ulster sent out more emigrants than any of the other three provinces. In 1842 a record 89,686 people left Ireland. The hope that home rule was imminent encouraged people to stay in Ireland in 1843, but the annual tally then began to rise again. In 1845, 75,000 people emigrated. There was no significant increase in emigration after the first potato crop failure in 1845, an event that was considered unlikely to be repeated in successive years, but when signs of blight appeared again in 1846, people began to look at emigration as a form of salvation, and just over 100,000 made the passage to Liverpool as a first stage in the journey to the US. Many of those did not have the passage money for the onward journey and opted to stay in Liverpool. By 1847, when people began to emigrate

JAMES HACK TUKE

His eyewitness testimony proved invaluable in bringing relief to the west of Ireland.

AN EMIGRANT SHIP, DUBLIN BAY,
1853, by Edwin Hayes, 1819–1904

in large numbers in order to flee the famine, with an estimated one million people flooding the city between January and April, Liverpool's welcome began to wear thin, faced with increasing numbers of starving, fever-stricken incomers, many of whom spoke only Irish.

By this time, Britain was in an economic downturn and offered few prospects. Many of those fleeing starvation and destitution began to look to the New World instead. There was some government assistance with fares to Canada and Australia, but only about 5 per cent of those who emigrated during the famine received official assistance – those who had been in workhouses for more than three months (in some cases they had to have been inmates for a year or more) could apply for assistance with their passage from the Poor Law rate. Others were offered financial incentives – passage and some money to help get them settled in their new lives – by their former landlords. The remainder were self-funding, using the 'American money' sent home by previous

PASSENGER ticket to a new life

emigrants. As hunger took hold, there was a busy
correspondence between those desperate to leave
and their émigré relatives – heartfelt requests
for funds usually received a generous response.
The British, hardened towards the Irish by a long

press campaign that portrayed them as bestial and unfeeling, were amazed by the response of Irish expatriots to the pleas of their countryfolk. The Quaker Samuel Tuke told a meeting of his coreligionists that

> [I]t is said that the Irish are reckless, yet a most interesting evidence of their thrift, their patriotism and their natural affection is to be seen in the remittances of the poor emigrants in America to their relations at home.

SAMUEL TUKE, Quaker philanthropist.

The profile of the emigrants was changing – previously almost exclusively young, male and single, the emigrants now included entire families, or several younger members of the same family, and, for the first time, young unaccompanied women.

In both Australia and the US, young women were in demand as servants. Most of those who travelled to Australia were orphans aged between 14 and 18 who had been sent from the workhouses under a scheme supported by the Colonial Office. In the two years from May 1848, 4,715 young girls were sent to Australia. They were accompanied on the long voyage (it lasted in the region of 100 days, the actual

A CATHOLIC PRIEST blesses kneeling emigrants as they prepare to leave their homes and families in Ireland for North America during the potato famine, around 1850.

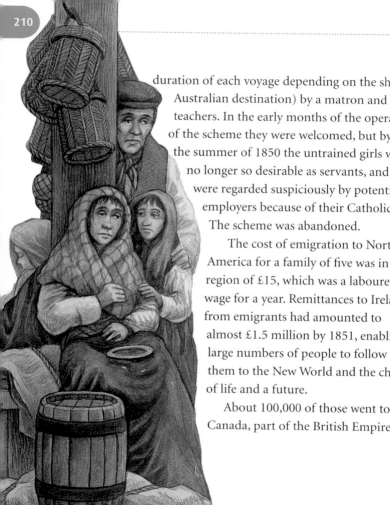

duration of each voyage depending on the ship's Australian destination) by a matron and teachers. In the early months of the operation of the scheme they were welcomed, but by the summer of 1850 the untrained girls were no longer so desirable as servants, and were regarded suspiciously by potential employers because of their Catholicism. The scheme was abandoned.

The cost of emigration to North America for a family of five was in the region of £15, which was a labourer's wage for a year. Remittances to Ireland from emigrants had amounted to almost £1.5 million by 1851, enabling large numbers of people to follow them to the New World and the chance of life and a future.

About 100,000 of those went to Canada, part of the British Empire and therefore readily accessible to other citizens of the empire. Fares to Canada were kept low to encourage people not to settle in Britain, where, increasingly, the Irish were unwanted. On that route some passengers' fares were subvented by landlords keen to clear their land, who also held out the promise of funds with which to start a new life in Canada. British ships sailing to Canada (and the US) were badly regulated and conditions were poor. They were very overcrowded, sometimes carrying twice the number of passengers that could be safely accommodated, food was sporadically distributed and inadequately cooked, and the holds were infested with lice, causing typhus to spread rapidly in the cramped unventilated holds. A few days into the voyage the water quality deteriorated and, in some cases, ran out long before the ship reached its destination. There was no requirement for the ships to have a doctor on board. The journey was long, lasting from six weeks to three months, depending on wind and weather conditions. The steerage

EMIGRATING FAMILY huddle aboard ship en route to America.

passengers were confined below decks, with no beds or mattresses and little ventilation – many suffered from diarrhoea and seasickness, but there was no sanitation or washing facilities. The stench was appalling and fever and infections spread rapidly.

Many of the passengers were half-starved and suffering from fever when they embarked, although they were supposed to pass a medical inspection. The rigours of the journey weakened them further and many died en route, their bodies thrown overboard with no funeral rites. The death rate was so high the ships became known as 'coffin ships'.

On arrival in Canada the passengers were supposed to disembark at the quarantine facility at Grosse Île in the St Lawrence River, 30 miles from the city of Quebec, but the authorities there were completely unprepared for the influx of sick passengers. The huge numbers had soon overwhelmed the facility and people were left on board until space could be made for them. By the summer of 1847 the line of ships waiting for disembarkation orders was several miles long. Many of those who had still been healthy on arrival succumbed to typhus in the cramped confines of the boats during the long delay. When they died, their bodies were dumped unceremoniously into the river. Dreadfully ill passengers were put into small tenders and landed on the beach, left to crawl to the quarantine facility, which was too full to take any more. The authorities quickly built wooden huts, but with hardly any medical attention and few staff, the death rate was high. The victims were buried in mass graves. Five thousand people were buried at Grosse Île in that dreadful year, accounting for 25 per cent of the 20,000 who died on the journey to Canada. More than half of the men who survived made their way to the US, despite the promised financial assistance of the landlords failing, in most cases, to materialise.

The journey to Australia, although longer, was considerably less hazardous than that to Canada or the US, even though those travelling to that far-flung outpost of the British Empire also embarked on

THE DUNBRODY carried passengers on the outward leg to North America between April to September from 1845 to 1851.

British ships. However, because the emigrants were subsidised by the government shipboard conditions were tightly controlled.

Those few who had sufficient funds to buy the more expensive passage on American vessels generally survived the trip. The ships were well regulated with a strictly enforced maximum number of passengers. The conditions and facilities on these ships was not due to any philanthropic motive, but stemmed from a desire to curb immigration from Ireland. The fever-ridden Catholic passengers were viewed with dismay by the settled Protestant populations of the Eastern seaboard of the US. However, those emigrants who landed in the US usually did well in the land of opportunity. Many stayed in the cities where they found menial work as servants and labourers, while others forged ahead to the frontier towns of the rapidly growing new country and made their lives there, making the most of the opportunity to start again. A contemporary ballad ('A New Song Called the Emigrant's Farewell

SHIPS left from ports in Ireland, bound for the US, Canada, Australia and elsewhere.

to Donegall') sums up the attitude of many emigrants:

> It was in the year of '46
> I was forced to leave my native land,
> To old Ireland I bid a long adieu
> And to my fond relations all.
> But now I'm in America
> No rents or taxes we pay at all,
> So now I bid a long farewell
> To my native land old Donegall.

An estimated one million people emigrated from Ireland during the famine years. In 1846 116,000 travelled to Canada and the US. The figure for 1847 was almost twice that. Between 1848 and 1850, 200,000 emigrated annually. Most went to English-speaking countries, although a few went as far as South America. In 1845 the population of Ireland was 8.5 million. By 1851, starvation, disease and emigration had reduced it to 6.5 million. As emigration continued after the famine, the population of Ireland continued to shrink and has not regained its pre-famine levels.

The Legacy of the Famine

We are a vibrant first-world country, but we have a humbling third-world memory.
Irish President, Mary McAleese, 1997

Any event or combination of circumstances that reduces the population of a country by 25 per cent will never be forgotten. The effects of the Great Famine were far-reaching, establishing a pattern of emigration, population decline and a distrust of the administration on a scale never before experienced.

Even after the potato blight had disappeared, hunger was endemic and evictions continued. There were regular food shortages caused by crop failure, but the emergencies were localised and had little effect on population levels. However, emigration continued apace (it didn't really tail off until the 1990s), and by 1911, the population of the island of Ireland had dwindled by a further 2,000,000 from 6,500,000 in 1850 to less than 4,500,000. In England and Wales in the same period the population doubled. By the 1960s the population of the island of Ireland stood at around 4,000,000. The marriage age soared from 24 years and four months for women and 27 years and seven months for men in 1840, to 28–29 years and 33 years respectively. With the practice of dower (whereby the bride's family gives a cash gift to the groom) increasing after the famine, the marriage rate also declined dramatically, with 25 per cent of Irish women never marrying.

The effects of the famine on the agricultural landscape of Ireland were unprecedented. During the famine, through forced evictions or so-called voluntary surrenders, 25 per cent of small farms (those that had fewer than 15 acres in total) disappeared, absorbed by the larger holdings. Many landowners, unable to pay their mortgages, sold their estates – by 1870 most of them had left and a new wave of landowners had arrived on the scene. Unlike their predecessors, many of these new landlords were Irish.

DERELICT COTTAGE, a common sight, especially in the west of Ireland

EMIGRANTS LEAVING Queenstown, Ireland, for New York, 1874. Queenstown, whose Irish name was Cobh, was the major Irish port of immigrant embarkation for North America.

Learning the lesson of dependence on a single crop, small farmers began to plant several different crops each year in order to be sure of a food supply. A new system of land inheritance was introduced. Before the famine, farmers bequeathed their land to their sons, to be shared equally. In the period of rising birth rates that preceded the Great Famine, this meant that modest plots of land were subdivided into smaller and smaller fields incapable of sustaining a family. After the famine it was generally only the eldest son who inherited, leaving his siblings to find other means of livelihood after their father's death, and it was this more than anything else that caused the persistence of emigration for more than another century. Emigrants continued

A LETTER FROM AMERICA

Young woman reading a letter from a relative in the US to an older woman outside a thatched stone cottage.

to send remittances to the families they left behind, in many cases funding farm improvements and the purchase of livestock, allowing younger children in the family to receive an education and sisters to have the dowries that enabled them to marry. They also sent money for the building and refurbishment of Catholic churches in their newly devout home country.

In 1860, the *Times* of London published a prescient assessment of what continuing emigration would mean.

> If this goes on as it is likely to go on … an Ireland there will still be, but on a colossal scale, and in a new world. We shall only have pushed the Celt westwards. Then, no longer cooped between the Liffey and the Shannon, he will spread from New York to San Francisco and keep up the ancient feud at an unforeseen advantage … We must gird our loins to encounter the nemesis of seven centuries' misgovernment. To the end of time a hundred million spread over the largest habitable area in the world, and, confronting us everywhere by sea and land, will remember that their forefathers paid tithe to the Protestant clergy, rent to the absentee landlords, and a forced obedience to the laws which these had made.

IRISH IMMIGRANTS

disembarking at New York, 1855

Emigration and famine memory evoked strong nationalist feelings in the Irish communities that had formed in cities across the globe, especially in the US. Most of those fleeing the famine arrived in the US penniless and were unable to move on from the cities where they landed, leading to large

Irish populations in the US cities of the Eastern seaboard – by 1860, in the cities of Boston, Baltimore, New York and Philadelphia, 25 per cent of the population was Irish. Life for the unskilled emigrants was hard, their living conditions were poor and crowded and, until their children began to achieve success in their adoptive country, they remained at the bottom of the heap socially. Encouraged by the bitter rhetoric and agitation of nationalists such as John Mitchel and other leaders of the Young Ireland movement who had fled to the US after the failure of the rebellion of 1848, they provided a good medium for the germination of a hatred against the British administration that would come to a head in the failed Fenian rebellion of 1867. Irish emigrants continued to provide financial support to the movement for Irish freedom and preserved a romantic attachment to Ireland through organisations such as the Ancient Order of Hibernians and the Friendly Sons of Saint Patrick. Although St Patrick's Day had been celebrated in some parts of America since the first half of the 18th century, it was after the major famine emigration that it became a regular occurrence. The rousing keynote speeches delivered at the annual St Patrick's Day parades were soon focusing on the oppression of the Irish people by the British and calling for donations towards the heroic struggle this necessitated. Funding continued to come from the US, providing resources for the 1916 Rising and for the nationalist cause during the subsequent Troubles in Northern Ireland.

The decline of the Irish language is often blamed on the Great Famine, but this is not entirely true. The rate of decline was accelerated as a result of the death toll during the famine, and through emigration both during and after the famine, but the numbers of Irish speakers had been reducing in the decades of the first half of the 19th century. It is estimated that in 1800 around 40 per cent of the population spoke Irish as their everyday language. By 1845, this had been revised to 30 per cent. Socio-economic status determined whether people spoke Irish or English as their first language – it is striking that the leading nationalist agitators in the 18th and 19th centuries came from the middle or upper classes and spoke English. English was the language of business and trade, and Irish speakers were concentrated in the poorer parts of the country, those parts that were most depopulated owing to death and emigration during and after the Great Famine.

By 1861, only 24 per cent of the population was Irish-speaking, and the decline continued until 1926, when only 18 per cent, most of whom lived in the more isolated rural areas, predominantly in the west of Ireland, described themselves as Irish speakers. This figure would probably have been lower but for the foundation of Conradh na Gaeilge, the Gaelic League, in 1893 in an attempt to revive the language and slow down the increasing Anglicisation of the country. (One of the founders of the league, and its first president, was Douglas Hyde, who would later be the first professor of modern Irish at UCD, and the first president of Ireland.) Although Irish is a compulsory subject in schools in the Republic of Ireland it is spoken in very few homes, and only about 33 per cent of the

DOUGLAS HYDE (in back of car holding top hat), leaving Dublin Castle with a cavalry escort following his 1938 inauguration as Ireland's first president.

population today has any proficiency, with just 3 per cent speaking the language fluently.

After more than one and a half centuries the Great Irish Famine is viewed largely with disbelief – how could so many could have died from starvation and its associated diseases in the midst of plenty? John Mitchel and those like him fanned the flames of bitterness and resentment towards a British administration which, at best, was guilty of doing little to alleviate the increasingly dire situation of the distressed poor of its smaller island. Had the word 'genocide' existed during Mitchel's lifetime, he would doubtless have used it in relation to the policies that resulted in such a high mortality rate. Whether the deaths were the result of genocide, incompetence or negligence, the last word should, in justice, go to Máire Ní Dhroma, a resident of Rinn in Waterford during the famine years, who wrote a song challenging the popular idea that the famine was an act of Providence.

REILIG AN TSLÉIBE Famine Graveyard memorial to Máire Ní Dhroma

Amhrán na bPrátaí Dubha

Na prátaí dubha do dhein ár gcomharsana a scaipeadh orainn,
Do chuir sa phoorhouse iad is anonn thar farraige;
I Reilig an tSléibhe tá na céadta acu treascartha
Is uaisle na bFflaitheas go ngabhaid a bpáirt.
A Dhia na Glóire fóir agus freagair sinn,
Scaoil ár nglasa agus réidh ár gcás,
Is an bheatha arís ó Do Chroí go gcasair orainn,
Is an poorhouse go leagair anuas ar lár.
Más mar gheall ar ár bpeacaí claona tháinig an chéim seo eadrainn,
Oscail ár gcroí is díbir an ghangaid as;
Lig braon beag de Do fhíorspiorad arís chun ár gcneasaithe,
Is uaisle na bhFlaitheas go ré ár gcás.
Níl aon chuimhne againne oíche nó maidin Ort
Ach ar ainnise an tsaoil ag déanamh marbhna,
Is, a Íosa Críost, go dtógair dínn an scamall so
Go mbeimis dod amharcadh gach am den lá.
Tá na bochta so Éireann ag plé leis an ainnise,
Buairt is anacair is pianta báis,
Leanaí bochta ag béiceadh is ag screadadh gach maidin,
Ocras fada orthu is gan dada le fáil.

Ní hé Dia a cheap riamh an obair seo,
Daoine bochta a chur le fuacht is le fán,
Iad a chur sa phoorhouse go dubhach is glas orthu,
Lánúineacha pósta is iad scartha go bás.
Na leanaí óga thógfaidís suas le macnas
Sciobtaí uathu iad gan trua gan taise dhóibh:
Ar bheagán lóin ach súp na hainnise
Gan máthair le freagairt díbh dá bhfaighidís bás.
A Rí na Trua is a Uain Ghil Bheannaithe,
Féach an ainnise atá dár gcrá
Is ná lig ar strae Uait Féin an t-anam bocht
Is a fheabhas a cheannaigh Tú é féin sa Pháis.
Nach trua móruaisle go bhfuil mórán coda acu
Ag íoc as an obair seo le Rí na nGrás;
Fearaibh bochta an tsaoil seo ná fuair riamh aon saibhreas
Ach ag síorobair dóibh ó aois go bás.
Bíonn siad ar siúl ar maidin, ar an dóigh sin dóibh,
Is as sin go tráthnóna ag cur cuiríní allais díobh,
Níl aon mhaith ina ndícheall mura mbíd cuíosach, seasmhach,
Ach téigi abhaile is beidh bhúr dtithe ar lár.

The Song of the Black Potatoes

The black potatoes did our neighbours scatter from us,
Did put them in the poorhouse and away over the sea;
In the Graveyard of the Mountain hundreds of them are laid low
And the nobility of Heaven may they take their part.
O God of Glory shield and answer us,
Loosen our bonds and banish our grief,
And from Your Heart may You restore life again to us,
And the poorhouse may You bring down to the ground.
If it is on account of our perverse sins that we have come to this pass,
Open our hearts and drive the venom out of them;
Send a little drop of Your true spirit to heal us once again,
And the nobility of Heaven may they end our distress.
By morning or night we do not remember You
As we lament the wretchedness of life,
And, O Jesus Christ, may You take this cloud from us
That we may look on You at all times of the day.
These poor people of Ireland are facing misery,
Sorrow and hardship and the pains of death,
Poor children are bawling and screeching each morning,
A long hunger is on them and there's nothing to get.

It was not God who ever planned this business,
To expose poor people to cold and wandering;
To put them in the poorhouse to mourn in captivity,
Where married couples are kept apart till they die.
The young children they would have raised in gladness,
Were snatched from them without pity or regard:
Their meagre fare just the soup of sadness
With no mother to answer them when they died.
O King of Pity, O Bright Blessed Lamb,
Look at the misery that afflicts us
And do not permit the poor soul to stray from You
That You bought so dearly on the Cross.
Pity the grandees who have everything
When they pay the King of Graces for this;
The poor people of this world never had anything
But work without end till they died.
So they are on their feet in the morning,
They pour out their sweat until dusk,
Their best is no use unless quiet and unflagging,
Just knock off and your homes will get bust.

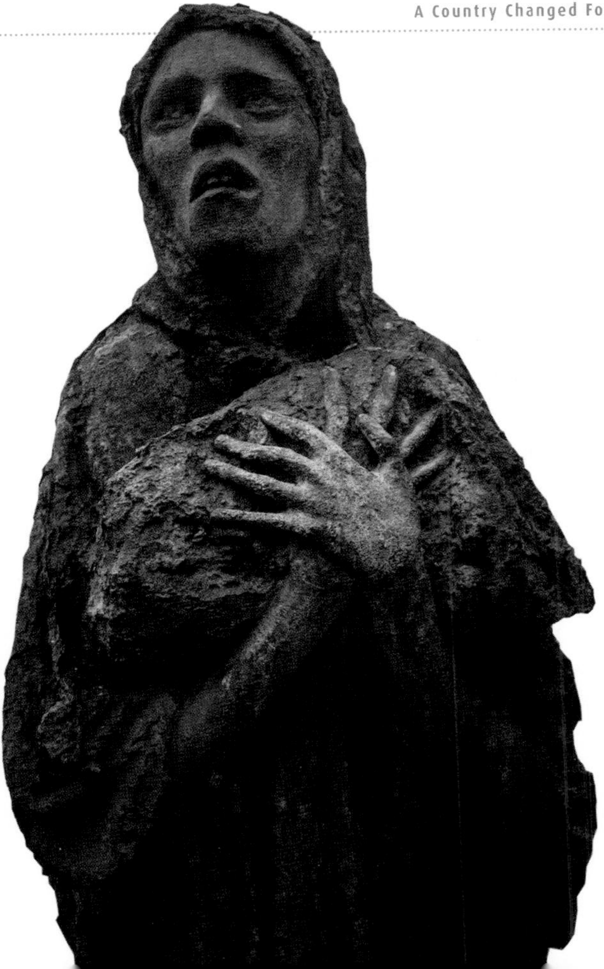

Chapter 12: Memory and Memorial

How the Great Famine has been Commemorated

The dead are not far from us ... they cling in some strange way to what is most still and deep within us.

W. B. Yeats

For well over a century after the famine there was little commemoration of those who had died and were exiled during the dreadful years. There were no obvious heroes to acclaim, no uprisings, no military engagements to celebrate. The centenary of the famine years coincided with the ending of the Second World War – it was a period of economic hardship in the new Republic of Ireland, with some food shortages. Ireland was dependent on its nearest neighbour and the administration may have been loath to antagonise Britain by marking the anniversary of a horror that could have been mitigated by that same administration's predecessors at Westminster.

Whatever the reason, it was not until the mid-1990s, the 150th anniversary of the Great Famine, that the memorialising of the famine began in earnest. Until then, public memorials had been few and far between, and included Edward Delaney's 1964 bronze in St Stephen's Green, Dublin. His *Famine Memorial* was conceived in conjunction with a monument to Wolfe Tone. It comprises three elongated figures who emanate an almost palpable misery. It also includes a dog, perhaps a reference to the scavenging dogs who feasted on the unburied or inadequately buried corpses during the famine years.

More than 100 monuments were created in Ireland during the 1990s, and many were also erected in the places that became centres of the famine diaspora, from Canada to the US to Australia. Many of those monuments were centred on the Celtic High Cross. The 1,300,000 Irish emigrants who passed through Liverpool

FAMINE MEMORIAL
St Stephen's Green, Dublin, by Edward Delaney

en route to the New World are commemorated on a monument to the victims of the Blitz.

The monuments range from statues to sculpture installations, to museums, such as Doagh Visitor Centre and Famine Museum and Donaghmore Famine Museum, to simple plaques – some remember particular events, others commemorate the famine period as a whole. The challenge has been to create places of remembrance, rather than famine theme parks that entice visitors with the prospect of a family day out. (There are too many famine memorials to include here, but a full list of memorials in Ireland and worldwide is available on www.irishfaminememorials.com.)

The Famine Museum at Strokestown Park, Strokestown, Co. Roscommon, Ireland is twinned with the Irish Memorial National Historic Site, Grosse Île, Quebec, Canada. (More than 5,500 Irish who emigrated during the famine are buried in the mass graves at Grosse Île.) Opened in 1994, the museum is located in the stable block of the 'Big House' once owned by the Pakenham Mahon family, a juxtaposition that highlights the landlordism that was one of the reasons for the famine, and its dreadful consequences. It is a fitting monument – 1,490 tenants on the estate were offered the choice of emigration, starvation or incarceration in the poorhouse.

They walked along the Royal Canal from Strokestown to the Dublin docks, a journey of 155 kilometres (about 100 miles) where their landlord had bought them passage on four cargo ships (filled with Irish grain) bound for Quebec. About half of the Strokestown emigrants died before they reached Canada. They are said to have been the biggest group given so-called assisted passage, and they are known as the 'missing 1,490'.

There are no surviving artefacts of the tenants' lives at Strokestown, but a huge archive of documents was discovered by the present owner of the house, and these were used as the basis for the museum.

In 1997 sculptor Rowan Gillespie's bronze, *Famine*, was

A LOCK on the Royal Canal

donated to the state by Norma Smurfit, who had commissioned it privately. Installed on Custom House Quay, Dublin, a point of departure for emigrants during the famine, it depicts six life-sized emaciated people and a dog, and it is easy to imagine that they might be six of the 'missing 1,490' of Strokestown. Unlike those famine memorials that depict families, this sculpture shows no connection between the six figures, a reflection of the fact that many emigrants travelled alone, either because they were alone in the world or were necessarily

ROWAN GILLESPIE'S bronze installation on Custom House Quay

separated from whatever family members were still alive. The dog is reminiscent of Edward Delaney's St Stephen's Green memorial.

Also at Custom House Quay, near Rowan Gillespie's installation, a replica of the *Jeanie Johnston* is docked. Not a memorial in the strict sense of the word, it provides visitors with a second-hand experience of being an emigrant to the New World. The original *Jeanie Johnston* was built in 1847 in Quebec as a cargo ship, but the company that owned her began to carry emigrants from Ireland to North America, beginning on 24 February 1848, with 193 passengers. Her 16 seven-week voyages over the next six years brought 2,500 Irish emigrants to North America. Not a single person died on any of those voyages.

The famine monument at Murrisk in Westport, County Mayo, designated the National Famine Monument, occupies an unrivalled position with panoramic views over Clew Bay. The striking bronze sculpture by John Behan depicts a boat, a 'coffin

JEANIE JOHNSTON
A replica of the original ship which made 16 emigrant journeys to North America between 1847 and 1855

ship'. The three masts silhouetted starkly against the landscape call to mind the three crosses of the Crucifixion. The rigging is populated with skeletal figures, with more clinging to the sides of the ship. The coffin ships that left Ireland packed with emigrants, many of whom did not survive the voyage, are emotive emblems of the famine, and it is easy to see why this particular sculpture has been chosen as the national monument, although the incidence of onboard deaths was not actually very high, relative to the numbers of emigrants who reached their destinations alive.

In Newmarket, County Kilkenny, Gáirdin an Ghorta

NATIONAL FAMINE
memorial designed by Irish artist John Behan, portrays a coffin ship full of dying people.

(the Famine Garden), which opened in 1999, takes visitors through the famine, beginning the journey in a representation of a thatched cottage and moving through various spaces dedicated to suffering, for example the Bridge of Hardship and the Valley of Sorrows, finishing up in the Garden of Hope and Reconciliation.

In 1995 *An Gorta Mór*, a monument dedicated to all who lost their lives in the Great Famine was erected in the grounds of the workhouse at Ennistymon, County Clare. It was commissioned by the Ancient Order of Hibernians and Clare County Council and was executed by Kerry artist Alan Ryan Hall. It is believed that 20,000 people died in the Ennistymon workhouse, many of them children, and they were buried in

AN GORTA MÓR, a monument in the grounds of the workhouse at Ennistymon, County Clare.

the workhouse grounds without being afforded the basic dignity of a shroud or coffin.

The memorial consists of two workhouse doors, with a small boy seeking entry at the right-hand door. The left-hand door shows the anguished face of a woman, presumably his mother, and a pair of disembodied, clenched hands. The sculpture is based on an extract from the minutes of the Board of Guardians for the Ennistymon Union, and reproduces a note pinned to the shirt of an orphan who was found at the workhouse door on the morning of 25 February 1848. The note, the text of which is reproduced on the memorial, read:

Gentlemen,

There is a little boy named Michael Rice of Lahinch aged about 4 years. He is an orphan, his father having died last year and his mother has expired on last Wednesday night, who is now about to be buried without a coffin!! Unless ye make some provision for such. The child in question is now at the Workhouse Gate expecting to be admitted, if not it will starve.

Rob S. Constable

On a freezing night in the winter of 1849, 600 starving people set out from Louisburgh, County Mayo, to walk the 25 kilometres (15 miles) to their landlord's hunting lodge at Delphi. They had been told that the council of workhouse guardians would be there and would give them food. No food was provided, and many of the 600 died on the walk back – some were found by the shore of Lake Doolough with grass in their mouths. The Doolough Tragedy Memorial is simple and understated – a plain stone cross inscribed with the words 'Doolough Tragedy 1849: Erected to the memory of those who died in the famine of 1845–49'. At the base of the cross is a plaque that reads: 'To commemorate the hungry poor who walked here in 1849 and walk the Third World today. Freedom for South Africa 1994. How can men feel themselves honoured by the humiliation of their fellow beings'. People have walked this route in memory since 1988. Bishop Desmond Tutu, the children of Chernobyl, the Choctaw Nation and the Cellist of Sarajevo are just a few of those who have joined the

THE DOOLOUGH
Tragedy Memorial

ordinary people of Ireland on their commemorative pilgrimage.

Three monuments were commissioned in Sligo in 1997 after a famine graveyard was discovered during excavations at St John's Hospital in Ballytivnan, outside Sligo town. The Sligo Famine Committee decided that the site should be honoured and that the buildings for which it had been excavated would not be built there. *Faoin Sceach*, a stylised windswept tree with bare branches, executed by sculptor Fred Conlon, was installed on the site. The inscription reads:

> This Bronze Tree stands as a symbol of dignity. It commemorates the un-named dead of this area who perished in the Great Famine of 1845–1847. An Gorta Mór was like a never-ending winter, its chill of desolation brought hunger, disease and death. In Ireland the lone tree of 'Sceach' was held in a position of high importance from early Celtic mythology to recent times. The boulder stones surrounding

BRONZE 'LONE TREE' sculpture commemorates those who died in the Great Hunger in Ireland, 1845–51 and stands as a memorial over their mass grave in Sligo.

the base allude to ancient forms of burial.

Mar sceach fé thathaint na gaoithe
Tá m'anam á lúbadh anocht*
Seán Ó Riordáin, 1817–77
*Like a tree blown in the wind,
My soul bends tonight

IRON GATE
featuring stylised human faces marks the entrance to a famine graveyard in Sligo, Ireland.

St. John's Hospital is also the location for a set of gates designed and made by Niall Bruton leading to the famine graveyard. The inscription outside the graveyard reads:

Reilig an Ghorta Mhóir

You are entering a long abandoned Famine Graveyard. Here, on the grounds of County Sligo's 1841 Workhouse, lie buried the ravaged bones of unnumbered thousand nameless souls—

'I witnessed the women and little children, crowds of whome were to be seen scattered

over the turnip fields, like a flock of famished crows, devouring the raw turnips, mothers half naked, shivering in the snow and sleet, uttering exclamations of despair whilst their children were screaming with hunger … The workhouse is full, and police are stationed at the doors to keep the numberous applicants out …'
Captain Wynne, District Inspector,
Christmas Eve, 1846

Unfed, unwashed, unmourned,
Here lie the remains.
To we, the survivors, the sacred rite of burial,
Into our hands their trampled bones, perpetual vigil.

In Sligo town centre, at the quays from where 30,000 people emigrated between 1847 and 1851, there is another sculpture by Niall Bruton, *Famine Family*, a representation of a grieving family of three, parents and one child, a small girl. The inscription is a letter from an evicted father, representative of so many, begging for funds from his son, who had already emigrated to the US:

Letter to America, January 2, 1850

I am now I may say alone in the world all my brothers and sisters are dead and children but yourself… We are all ejected out of Lord Ardilaun's ground the times was so bad and all Ireland in such a state of poverty that no person could pay rent. My only hope now rests with you, as I am without one shilling and as I said before I must either beg or go to the poorhouse … I remain your affectionate father Owen Larkin be sure answer this by return of post

THE FAMINE FAMILY, a sculpture by Niall Bruton, Sligo

At its base, the memorial includes W. B. Yeats's haunting line – 'The dead are not far from us … they cling in some strange way to what is most still and deep within us.'

In County Roscommon the bronze sculpture *An Gorta Mór* by Elizabeth McLaughlin depicts an emaciated standing trio, a mother and two children, based on one of the many illustrations of famine victims that appeared in the *Illustrated London News*. The statue, located in the Famine Memorial Garden on the site of the Roscommon workhouse, was unveiled in 1999.

In Clones, County Monaghan, the *Famine Memorial*, a bronze by sculptor Carolyn Mulholland, is located in the famine graveyard in the former workhouse cemetery. The life-sized, shrouded figure, representing all those who died, lies on a stone slab as if on a bier. An extract from an 1846 report in the *Fermanagh Reporter* is roughly scratched into the bronze surface.

> It would be impossible to exaggerate the awful destitution that exists in the town of Clones and neighbourhood. No day passes but some victims of this frightful calamity are committed to the grave. The workhouse contains upwards of a hundred over the regulated number and most of them were all but starved before they obtained admission. Their exhausted frames were then unable to bear the food doled out to them and hence they are, at this moment, dying in dozens.

The Famine Warhouse is an unusual combined memorial in Ballingarry, County Tipperary. The McCormack Farmhouse, often referred to as Widow McCormack's House, was scene of the 1848 Young Ireland rebellion, one of several in Europe's Year of Revolutions. William Smith O'Brien led a group of rebels who besieged the farmhouse, where 47 policemen had blocked themselves in, taking the five children of the family hostage. The house is now a museum with an exhibition on the 1848 Rebellion and the history of the Great Famine and emigration.

WIDOW MCCORMACK'S House, Ballingarry, County Tipperary

In Limerick City, the *Broken Heart Fountain*, unveiled in 1997, is a bronze sculpture by Maria Pizzuti at Steamboat Quay. Representing a large, broken heart, the sculpture is dedicated to 'the thousands of people who used this site as a holding station in the famine of 1854 to 1849 prior to emigration to the new world never to return'. Designed to be a water feature, the basin in which it sits is now dry and the sculpture looks abandoned and derelict.

Skibbereen in West Cork, the place acknowledged to have been the worst affected by the Great Famine, failed in its efforts to be the location of the National Famine Memorial. The memorial is in Abbeystrowry graveyard, the burial site of between 9,000 and 11,000 victims of the famine. Five limestone standing stones, arranged around one end of the famine 'pit', honour those who came to the aid of the residents of Skibbereen. In 1847 Lord Dufferin gave a vivid description of the horror.

ABBEYSTROWRY graveyard, site of the burial of over 9,000 famine victims

> By these graves no service had been performed, no friends had stood, no priest had spoken words of hope and of future consolation in a glorious eternity! The bodies had been daily thrown in, many without a coffin, one over another, the uppermost only

IN MEMORY
OF THE VICTIMS OF
THE FAMINE 1845-48
WHOSE COFFINLESS BODIES
WERE BURIED IN THIS PLOT

Go ndéana Dia trócaire ar a nanamacha

hidden from the light of day by a bare three inches of earth, the survivors not even knowing the spot where those most dear to them lay sleeping.

A plaque on the wall of the cemetery reads:

Happier were the victims of the sword
than the victims of hunger
who pined away, stricken by
want of the fruits of the field.

Although signs of the famine in Northern Ireland are present in the shape of workhouse graveyards and famine roads, monuments to those who died during the Great Famine are few and far between. A notable exception is Eamonn O'Doherty's *Famine Memorial* at Enniskillen, County Fermanagh, installed in 1996. It is a simple and eloquent installation – the flagstone floor and two gable ends of a small stone cottage provide a frame for a plain metal table topped with five empty dishes.

In 2013 Cork-based sculptor Alex Pentek was commissioned to create *Kindred Spirits*, a sculpture to commemorate the generosity of the Choctaw Nation of Oklahoma who donated $170 to Irish famine relief in 1847. At that time the Choctaw people were undergoing great hardship themselves, having been forced into exile and starvation, so the gift was extraordinarily generous. The metal sculpture was unveiled in June 2017, a graceful and majestic representation of nine 6-metre (20-foot) eagle feathers arranged in a circle and reaching skywards.

In 1847, Sultan Abdülmedjid of the Ottoman Empire, sent aid to Ireland, encouraged probably by his Irish physician, Justin Washington McCarthy from Cork. Initially, he pledged £10,000

CREATED BY ALEX PENTEK, *Kindred Spirits* remembers the aid given by the Chocktaw Nation during the Great Famine.

SULTAN ABDÜLMEDJID
Reigned 2 July 1839–2 June 1861

but was prevailed upon to to reduce it to £1,000, to avoid embarrassing Queen Victoria because she herself had given only £2,000.

The often recounted, but unsubstantiated story goes, that the Sultan secretly sent several shiploads of grain to Dublin, where they were refused permission to dock. They travelled up the coast to Drogheda, where the grain was unloaded and distributed. The Westcourt Hotel on West Street displays a plaque, unveiled in 1995, stating:

> In remembrance and recognition of the generosity of the People of Turkey towards the People of Ireland.

It must have seemed strange, and unlikely, to the British administration that faraway 'heathens' would make a more meaningful contribution to Irish famine relief than they themselves could even contemplate doing.

Select bibliography

Higgins, Michael D., *When Ideas Matter: Speeches for an Ethical Republic.* London: Head of Zeus Ltd, 2016

Mark-Fitzgerald, Emily. *Commemorating the Irish Famine: Memory and Monument.* Liverpool: Liverpool University Press, 2013.

O'Rourke, Canon John, *The History of the Great Irish Famine of 1847 – with Notices of Earlier Famines,* first published in 1874. The edition used as a reference here is published by Bibliobazaar, Charleston, SC.

Póirtéir, Cathal (ed.), *The Great Irish Famine* (The Thomas Davis Lecture Series). Cork: Mercier Press, 1995.

Tóibín, Colm and Ferriter, Diarmaid (eds.), *The Irish Famine: A Documentary.* London: Profile Books Ltd, 2001.

Picture credits